It's Who You Know

The Magic of Networking in Person
and on the Internet

It's Who You Know

The Magic of Networking in Person and on the Internet

Cynthia Chin-Lee

BookPartners, Inc.
Wilsonville, Oregon

Copyright 1998 by Cynthia Chin-Lee
All rights reserved
Printed in U.S.A.
Library of Congress Catalog 97-71613
ISBN 1-885221-71-1

Cover design by Richard Ferguson
Text design by Sheryl Mehary

This book may not be reproduced in whole or in part,
by electronic or any other means which exists or
may yet be developed, without permission of:

BookPartners, Inc.
P.O. Box 922
Wilsonville, Oregon 97070

*To Andy Pan, my loving husband
and biggest networking catch!*

Table of Contents

	Foreword	vii
	Preface	ix
	Acknowledgments	xi
1	Why You Need to Network	1
2	Making Opportunity	11
3	Sources for Networking	33
4	Informational Interviewing	79
5	Networking on the Internet	113
6	Using Electronic Mail, Listservs, and Usenet News	125
7	Finding Career Resources on the World Wide Web	137
8	Creating a Simple Web Site	147
9	Maximizing Your Networking	155
	Appendices	
	A HTML 3.2 Tags	167
	B Sample Web Site	177
	Suggested Reading	181
	Index	183

Foreword

There are three kinds of people in this world:
People who make things happen.
People who watch things happen.
People who get knocked over the head and then say, "What happened?"

Making contact with people, that is, networking, is one of the best ways to make things happen for yourself and your business. I believe this strongly and know that networking has been influential in the success of my company.

This book gives insights into how, when, and where to network. It will make you a more effective individual, no matter what your goals are. The author has shown how successful people network, not in a selfish, opportunistic way, but in a sincere, mutually beneficial way for the individual, the family, company, and community.

Happy networking!

    James G. Treybig
    Founder
    Tandem Computers, Inc.
    Cupertino, California

Preface

This book is a practical, step-by-step guide on how to make personal and business contacts critical to your success. Networking has become so popular that some have called it a new kind of Yuppie disease. Many people are suspicious of networking, labeling it as trendy and an overly vague term. However, if you know how to make the right contacts in the right ways, you can enhance your business and personal life significantly.

There is an old saying, "It's not what you know; it's who you know." That may sound simplistic at first. On closer examination, your success often depends on a subtle, but important blend of what you know and who you know. As one joke goes, you not only have to have know-how to get the job done, you also need to have know-who.

You have probably heard over and over to "study hard and get good grades," with the implicit promise that success would be yours. So you follow the formula of getting a good education and working hard, devoting years of diligent study to attaining a college or university diploma and to have letters, such as B.A., M.S., or Ph.D., appended to your name.

Yet you could still be missing something. What you might be missing is the other part of the formula, the who you know part. You don't have to be a politician to realize that personal contacts are frequently the key to a deal, the clincher in a contract, or the difference between being just another job applicant and getting the job. This book discusses how you can control who you know.

The process of making contacts is not for the faint of heart. Gear yourself for taking some personal and social risks and challenging some of your fundamental beliefs.

Remember that the results — greater personal effectiveness and success — are worth the effort and the risks. This process involves the marketing of a revolutionary and unique product, one that the world has never seen before: YOU.

Personal contacts are the number one way for people to find jobs. According to Richard Bolles, author of the career classic *What Color is Your Parachute?*, sixty-eight percent of all jobs are found through personal contacts. In comparison fifteen percent of jobs are found through agencies; nine percent of jobs are found through ads; and eight percent of jobs are found through other methods.

The United States and the world economies move along an uncharted course. If downsizing hasn't affected you personally, it has probably affected someone you know, a friend, co-worker, or family member. Whether you lost your job or held onto it, the news is clear: keep networking.

The Internet has brought unprecedented opportunities to network across the globe efficiently and inexpensively. We are living in an exciting time in the information revolution. I hope your networking, whether in person or on the Internet, will enrich and broaden your life.

Acknowledgments

I would like to thank these people in particular: Rand Richards and my brother-in-law Philip Hays for helping me launch my career as an author, Cindy Martin for her care and effort in editing this book from the early stages, and Thorn Bacon of BookPartners for his enthusiasm. Thanks to my other intrepid editors: Howard Fisher, Elizabeth Smith, Barbara Kern, Stacey Esser, and Bonnie Umphreys.

Special thanks to my family members for their support: Andy and Vanessa Pan, and Nancy and William Chin-Lee.

Finally, thanks to the following people for their encouragement and participation in this book: Michele Hill, Susan Almazol, Joyce Hendrickson, Selma Meyerowitz and Hari Dharan, Wanda Cavanaugh, Carolyn Broughton, Lisa Chan, Jaci Carson-Hunt, Mary Hamilton, Rick Liu, Sandra Hays, Moon Yuen, Peter Wilcox, Stacy Lippert, Barbara Erichsen, Cathy Drees, Pamela Bloch, Carol Cook, Bob Hartmann, Marlene Shigekawa, Leslie Smith, Ron Tucker, Catherine Gerrity, Tom and Hui Huang, Lars Rohrberg, Marianna Grossmann, Allison and Hossein Banisadr, Susan and Mohammed Banisadr, Donna Gerry, Dave Weir, Harry Tong, Deirdre Harrington, Joyce Oliver, Guy Haas, Anna Chennault, Leslie Davidson, Jennie Magid, Senator Hiram Fong, Dennis Nino, Greg Chew, Charles and Elaine Dunn, Betty Kwong, Janet Bein, Kirk and Patricia Strong, Janice McCormick, Jeanie Jew, Gaylene Garlitz, John Hamilton, David Sin, Roger Dearth, Joe Schrengohst, and Nancy Navarro.

Also thanks to these organizations: Tandem Toastmasters Club; Asian Business League of San Francisco; Asian Business League of Silicon Valley; Organization of Chinese Americans, San Mateo Peninsula Chapter; Main Library of Palo Alto, CA; Society for Technical Communication, Silicon Valley Chapter.

1

Why You Need to Network

> *Remember this, and also be persuaded of its truth — the future is not in the hands of fate, but in ourselves.*
>
> Jules Jusserand

What makes some people more successful than others? Is it appearance, intelligence, or hard work? Could it be a determination to succeed? While each of these factors may play a role in determining success, another critical factor may be the ability to make contacts. Networking — the art of making contacts — has been glorified and maligned but generally misunderstood.

This book demystifies the art of networking and gives you practical tips on putting networking to use. You can use networking for many purposes — selecting a career, changing your job, getting a promotion, relocating to a new town, starting a business, or finding companionship. A personal network is like a safety net beneath the high perch of the tightrope walker. It can save you from a bad fall should you lose your job, get demoted, or suffer a severe personal blow.

Networking may become more prevalent as times get tougher. Indeed, relying on your network can cushion you from a volatile economy and the dizzying pace of modern life. Whether you live in boom times or bust, there will always be stiff competition for the most coveted prizes in society: the best jobs, the best schools, the best neighborhoods. As you set your goals higher and higher, you will need to network.

A Networking Story: The Unemployed Harvard Graduate

A few years ago, a bright, young woman graduated with honors from Harvard University. Harvard is no backwoods place to attend college, but when she tried to get a job, many employers told her she was overqualified and underexperienced. She was shocked to find the truth about getting a job: you need experience to get a job, but if you've never had a job, how do you get experience? It was a classic Catch-22, a paradox in the practical world that makes a victim of every beginner.

This young woman entered the job market as just one more job seeker among thousands of graduates with a liberal arts degree. Despite her impressive academic credentials, she had no apparent marketable skills. Worse yet, as a baby boomer, she was competing with the largest number of college-educated job seekers this country had ever seen. Her frustration at her inability to find a reasonably challenging job galvanized her to look for new ways to get what she wanted. Networking proved extremely effective in her job search and was an exciting way to see more of the world through the eyes and experiences of others. Networking had a profound effect on the course of her career. Through networking, she got her first big break — the break that allowed her to move from menial and clerical jobs into the professional world. How do I know? That networker was me.

The Plateauing Trap

Like me, as a job seeker, you may find it hard to get your foot in the door. Even if you have considerable experience in a career that you've worked at for several years, you may be feeling stifled. Statistics show that you will reach your career plateau earlier than people did in previous decades. Judith Bardwick, psychologist and author of *The Plateauing Trap,* estimates that managers in a previous generation reached the highest levels in their careers in their late forties or early fifties. Today, a white male manager will peak in his early forties. The picture is more serious for women and minorities, who will reach their career peak in their late thirties. To resist the tendency to plateau, you can diversify your career through networking to get lateral transfers or career changes and continue to supplement your education as you grow older. Even if you cannot continue to be promoted, you do not have to stagnate.

Because of corporate cutbacks and the population growth trends (more people in the thirty to forty-five age range than ever before), more qualified candidates are competing for the top jobs. Betty Lehan Harragan, a syndicated career columnist, reports, "We have a much more competitive group looking for the same jobs. There used to be five people looking for a job. Now it's a hundred."

The message is clear that people are not able to get the jobs or promotions they want as easily as before, they are stagnating earlier, yet they have higher expectations. In a recent survey of a large, multinational corporation well-known for its people-oriented philosophy, forty-seven percent of the employees said they were unsatisfied in their careers. If you are a baby boomer, you probably have higher expectations but fewer opportunities than your parents had. Baby boomers are "likely to be an unhappy generation because their quality of life will be less than that of their parents.... They're likely to be somewhat downwardly mobile," reports Gary Dworkin, a University of Houston sociologist.

If you still have doubts about this gloomy forecast, these statistics from the Department of Labor and the Bureau of the Census should convince you. In the last decade, the number of graduates in the work force has increased more than 100 percent, but the total work force grew by only forty-one percent. This means that the job market has not grown enough to keep pace with the number of college-educated people in the work force. Salaries for college graduates have declined, and forty-seven percent of college graduates ages twenty-four and under are in jobs that do not require a college education.

Given this dismal scenario, networking has become a crucial strategy to supplement conventional job-seeking methods. Remember the "old boy network?" That phrase refers to the sons of blue-blood families. These young men attend exclusive preparatory schools in New England and are funneled to the Ivy League. After college or graduate school, these fellows take care of one another; they refer their former classmates to the top jobs and best opportunities on Wall Street, in government, and in Hollywood. Although you don't have to be one of the "old boys" to take advantage of the growing phenomenon of networking, you must be willing to learn and use networking techniques.

Networking Is Not a Panacea

Networking is not a panacea to solve all your career or personal problems, however. Neither does it replace education, experience, or hard work. You are fooling yourself if you think networking by itself will transform you from a corporate peon to a shooting star. Networking can only complement the skills, training, and experience you already have.

If you count on networking alone and expect your contacts to replace hard work, ability, and creativity, or if you only take from your network contacts but never give anything back, you are what I call a "networking barracuda." This take-but-never-give phenomenon has led some to label networking as a questionable job search technique. You are wise to realize that the most successful networking is mutual.

Networking also has ethical limits. You need to define how big of a favor you can accept without losing your integrity and independence. If someone gives you substantial help in getting a job, does the person now "own" you or can he pressure you to do something unethical? For most of us, networking will never pose such moral dilemmas, but you should consider your limits when giving and receiving networking help.

Your career is only one facet of your life, and networking is only one element of your career and personal development. If you need to get a job urgently, do not rule out other, more traditional, sources, such as job agencies, recruiters, newspaper ads, direct application, job fairs, and so on. Some of these methods may prove as effective as networking. Given the tough competition you face, the more resources you harness the better your chances of finding what you want.

Why Network?

If you are looking for a job, consider this fact: according to employment agencies, 80 percent of the job openings are not filled through the want ads or job postings. Instead, they're filled through personal contacts; that is, by word-of-mouth networking.

Many large corporations sponsor employee referral programs because they have learned that a person referred by a current employee has a better chance of succeeding. Moreover, paying an employee $500 to $1,000 for referring a reliable, hard-working employee is significantly less expensive than placing ads in major newspapers, advertising by radio, or hiring through a professional recruiter. One human resources manager put it bluntly: "We simply do not like to hire strangers." People prefer to hire people that they know or at least know of because it usually eliminates doubts about whether a person is reliable and honest.

Dr. Adele Scheele, author of *Skills for Success* and a leading advocate for networking, writes: "There are many different reasons for creating and maintaining connections to others and their organizations. Connecting gives us perspective about how we work, provides us with different approaches to problems and sharpens our ideas of what is important, relevant, or new. Contacts also release us from a feeling of dependence, allowing us to be bolder in our thinking because we are no longer afraid that ours is the only job in the entire system.... All told, connecting with others is enriching and life-giving, and assures us of endless possibility and opportunity."

Networking is appropriate when traditional methods have not worked to bring the desired change, promotion, or new challenge. Traditional methods do not work for everybody. A full-time independent consultant confided in me that she never gets results from conventional methods. All of her consulting contracts come by word-of-mouth, which is networking.

Networking has become a powerful grass-roots strategy for environmental movements, political campaigns, and charities. Volunteer groups have long used networking techniques to promote causes that improve our world. Networking empowers groups to spread their message and solve complex problems locally and globally.

Networking also can empower you as an individual. It is an important strategy for overcoming the obstacles to getting the job, promotion, or career that will use and develop your skills to their highest potential.

When you find yourself looking for some change, excitement, or a new challenge, networking can be surprisingly helpful and effective.

Make Your Own Contacts

When I was in college, I thought that if you worked hard and made good grades, you would eventually be rewarded with a good job and salary. I believed in Horatio Alger and in the merit system — that those who work hard are rewarded with success and prosperity.

My grandfather, a penniless Chinese peasant, came to the United States with limited skills and little education. By working hard at his modest laundry, he managed to raise a brood of kids and, with the help of the GI bill, sent most of them to college. I should note that, in addition to much hard work, my grandparents depended on a network that revolved around Chinatown and their extended clan, the Lee family. The Lees helped one another start small businesses, such as restaurants and laundries, and they formed their own family associations with credit unions, women's clubs, and community activities.

My parents' generation achieved professional status along with comfortable four-bedroom homes with family rooms and two-car garages in the suburbs. While our parents lived in the post-war boom, however, the baby boomer generation faces a highly competitive world, with a tightening economy that is whipsawed by the cross-currents of huge federal deficits, environmental disasters, and international competition. Succeeding at school is merely a start. To succeed in the real world, you need more than ability — you need contacts.

While contacts are key, not all of us have families or friends who are wealthy and well-connected. So what do we do? We make our own contacts.

I met Lars at a birthday lunch for one of my colleagues. To become a business analyst in a marketing organization, Lars told me he made his own contacts. When he was looking for a job and a career path in marketing, he called the vice president of marketing in a company he had researched. When the secretary would not let him through, he asked her to advise him as to who could give him the information he needed. When he subsequently contacted the woman who was suggested, he told her that the secretary of the vice president had recommended that he contact her. Says Lars, "Trust me. It works."

My college roommate, Betty, showed me how to make personal contacts that can influence your career success. Once, when I was a senior, Betty gave a dinner party. She borrowed the luxurious penthouse suite of the master of Quincy House. Betty invited two of her professors and their spouses, the Quincy House master and his wife, the son of the prime minister of Singapore, who was studying at Harvard Law School for the year, and me, her assistant in the kitchen.

I was both surprised and intrigued by my roommate's confident hosting skills. Betty cooked gourmet cuisine and served the dishes flawlessly. The table was set with the elegance of a formal affair: fine linens, formal china, crystal goblets, and silverware. The conversation at the dinner table hummed along in a friendly, animated way beneath the sparkle of a brass chandelier.

At that time, I would have been hard pressed to make a decent cup of instant soup, but Betty was whipping up Cantonese steamed rock cod with black bean sauce. She dazzled me with her culinary abilities, her savvy and sophistication. She understood the art of making contacts. Because Betty was preparing for a career in international law with a specialization in Asia, she needed strong recommendations from her professors; and naturally, a personal contact with the family of a high government official in Singapore could also further her career.

Betty did not wait for her professors to write her glowing recommendations for law school. She made sure that her contacts with important people were friendly and direct. At the tender age of twenty-two, she knew how to develop close, personal rapport with key people in a legitimate and socially acceptable way.

2

Making Opportunity

> *... Ask, and it shall be given you; seek, and ye shall find; knock, and it shall be opened unto you.*
> *For everyone that asketh receiveth; and he that seeketh findeth; and to him that knocketh it shall be opened.*
>
> Luke 11:9-10 (KJV)

In a speech on career planning, James G. Treybig, founder of Tandem Computers (now part of Compaq), said there are three kinds of people in the world:

People who make things happen.

People who watch things happen.

People who get knocked over the head and then say, "What happened?"

All of us want to see ourselves as productive and successful individuals who can make things happen. Yet, we cannot do it alone. To become a productive, successful individual, we need contacts. At different times in our lives we need a mentor to help clarify our vision, a big brother or sister to goad us into action. Personal contacts can supply that little piece of information that helps us land the big contract or start our own business.

What is a Network?

According to Webster's *New Collegiate Dictionary,* a network is "a fabric or structure of cords or wires that cross at regular intervals and are knotted or secured at the crossings." A network is "an interconnected or interrelated chain, group, or system."

As part of a global network, all of us are interconnected in a system. We are not at the last rung of a ladder or at the lower tier of a hierarchy. Instead, we are members of a multidimensional web, with connections that can take us in multitudinous directions. Networks are not new; they exist in many different environments.

A simple and familiar network is a spider's web: delicate white filaments carefully arranged by an artistic arachnid. Consider how strong and flexible a spider's web can be, allowing the spider to ensnare its unsuspecting prey with little effort. Through its nearly invisible, but shimmering web, a spider can attract and catch prey many times larger than itself.

Similarly, the nets of a fisherman are merely ropes tied together to form a lattice, but they reap a generous bounty of seafood. The fishing industry discovered the power of a network many centuries ago. Instead of waiting long hours behind a fishing pole for one or two fish, fishermen cast their large nets to the sea to capture hundreds or thousands of fish.

Consider the powerful computer networks available to an employee in a giant, multinational corporation. You now can access databases and other forms of information stored all over the world through the electronic connection of computers, with split-second ease. Networking in the computer industry means being able to communicate electronically around the world and having access to vast information databases, such as the Library of Congress, United Press International (UPI), and the New York Stock Exchange.

Our era has been dubbed the age of information. Thus, the networker uses information, rather than natural resources or materials, to become more productive and effective. Networking today, exchanging ideas and information, creates a powerful synergy. You can achieve your goals more quickly and effectively if you know how to network with the right people, and they can accomplish their objectives more quickly and effectively by networking with you.

Networking, of course, cannot do everything for you. You still have to have a solid base of skills and abilities. Education and hard work are usually the starting points in any successful career. Networking is like the wind beneath your wings. It can give you the lift to make your career fly, but you still must do the flapping.

To be successful at networking, keep in mind these key principles:
- Openness and flexibility
- Goal orientation
- Self-disclosure
- Altruism and empowerment
- Gratitude
- Persistence

By developing these characteristics, you significantly increase your chances of making effective personal contacts.

Openness and Flexibility

The single-most important principle of networking is to have an open mind along with open ears and eyes. Many opportunities will present themselves to you, but you must not only be able to recognize them, you must also follow up on them. Dare to follow your dream! You meet many people in your lifetime; some you brush up against casually and others you work with every day. You will not become best friends with every person you meet, whether at a cocktail party or waiting in line at the grocery store. You can, however, observe the people you meet in every encounter and use the information from each contact, whether it is your relative visiting from out of town or a new co-worker or neighbor. Some minuscule piece of information might be the key to your next job or promotion.

Rosabeth Kanter, author of *The Change Masters,* recommends that we take a "kaleidoscopic" look at the world. A kaleidoscope is a small tube that uses mirrors to reinterpret a view in different patterns. By mixing and matching people and ideas, jumbling up times and places, you can recombine facts and data in a creative and new way. In networking, you make an acquaintance and perhaps months or years later, you renew the personal contact in a new place or for another purpose.

For example, as a high school student, I took a tour of the Capitol in Washington, D.C., with students from around the country. I made friends with some kids from Hawaii, so I tagged along when they went to visit one of the United States senators from Hawaii. The senator, then in his late sixties, was quite the gentle and friendly statesman you would expect. He told us to look him up when any of us were in Hawaii.

I took that suggestion literally and looked the senator up four years later when I attended the University of Hawaii as a graduate student. You might think I had *chutzpa* to reintroduce myself to the now retired United States senator, so I should explain that I had some advantages. My father, who was active in politics on the East Coast, was an acquaintance of the senator, and we shared a common ethnic heritage.

A letter was sent to the senator when I arrived in Hawaii, an appointment was made to meet him, and I was delighted to be warmly accepted. Later, the senator and his wife invited me to their son's birthday extravaganza held at their large estate with a private beach and swimming pool. It was like *Lifestyles of the Rich and Famous,* with waiters serving tropical coolers, chefs preparing roast suckling pig, and an open sushi bar.

I was introduced to my host's nephew, an attorney, who had just returned from Taiwan, the Republic of China. I casually asked whether he planned to visit the other China, the People's Republic of China. He replied that he would when his friend from San Francisco completed the hotel he was building there. As a student of East Asian languages, I found this exciting information and fantasized about the possibilities of working on such a project. Because of those possibilities, remote as they were at the time, I remembered to ask him for his business card.

This conversation probably lasted no longer than a few minutes, but it yielded a small piece of information that altered my career. Several months later, I decided to take a leave of absence from graduate school and to move to San Francisco. I called the attorney and asked his permission to contact his friend. When he graciously granted his permission, I asked for the details of his friend's name, address, and phone number. After arriving in California, I talked to the hotel developer and got my first real job, as a purchasing agent and translator. Networking paid off early in my career; I was able to get my first job and many subsequent opportunities through making personal contacts.

In *Working Woman* magazine, Cynthia Crossen characterizes networking as hard or soft. She writes that the "glad-handing style of formal professional networks" is heavy-handed. On the other end of the spectrum, getting ahead with a little help from your friends is considered soft networking. Hard networking is obvious and intentional while soft networking is subtle, even accidental. According to Crossen, getting opportunities through networking with your friends is "networking of the highest order — soft, serendipitous."

Many of us hear about new opportunities — we may even daydream about them — but we simply fail to follow through. I recently had coffee with a new acquaintance, a chemistry professor at a local university. When I told her I was a technical writing consultant, her face lit up as she replied, "I'd love to do some consulting on the side; my salary as a professor just isn't enough." I proceeded to tell her about some free-lance work that she could do, but she took no notes and didn't ask for my business card. She had a wonderful opportunity to learn about possible part-time contract work, but she failed to follow up. The professor was initially open to the new possibilities but, all too soon, she seemed to close her mind. It was a networking opportunity wasted.

Career consultant Adele Scheele advises us to be "open to new situations" to see where they might lead. She says that such experiences cultivate a sense of opportunity, of where and when and, most important, how to act in dif-

Making Opportunity

ferent situations. This openness and flexibility makes it all the more likely that something interesting or instructive will happen.

In addition to being open to new and interesting information, be flexible in terms of how you use the information from a personal contact. Consider this story: Bob was a young engineer at a manufacturing company. When his manager decided to leave management and return to being an individual contributor, Bob was asked to interview potential management candidates. He interviewed Carol, a manager from a local competitor. He found her to be dynamic and talented, and recommended to upper management that she be hired as the manager of his work group. As things turned out, she was not hired.

Bob was disappointed by his company's decision, but he decided to stay in contact with Carol. Within a few months, she became a manager at a young high tech company. By this time, Bob had confided in Carol that he was not happy at his present employer, so she jumped at the chance to hire him.

Bob's new company, one of the most successful start-up companies in history, reached a billion dollars in sales in just six years. Bob was flexible; he didn't write off Carol because she was not hired by his original company. Because of his flexibility, he got a rare opportunity to join a start-up company with generous stock options.

Opportunities do not necessarily come packaged the way you think they will. Be aware of the people around you, whether they are fellow party-goers or people you are interviewing for a job. Your next boss, a new friend, or future spouse could be there.

Goal Orientation

To make the most out of networking, you should have an idea of what your goals are and understand the general direction of your life, even if you do not know all the specific steps of the journey. In fact, you should never try to map out your life in detail because you might miss a grand adventure. However, you should have a goal established, such as finding a job, getting a promotion, changing your career, or starting a partnership. You need to know the direction you want to go, but be flexible in your approach to accomplishing the goal.

In goal-setting, pick the area in which you want to target your search. If you have recently graduated from school or are interested in many fields, you can target several different areas. Having more than a few areas of interest does not mean you are unstable, as one prospective employer once assessed me. On the contrary, you are probably open-minded and flexible; I learned from my father's example that you can have many careers simultaneously or serially. My father has been a medical doctor, teacher, political candidate, real-estate developer, community volunteer, administrator, and a dad, in various combinations throughout his long career.

However, do realize that if you target more than two or three fields, you are increasing your work load proportionally. Be realistic about your time and energy and set priorities so you don't spread yourself too thin. Remember, looking for a job takes the same effort and energy as a full-time job.

Planning a career requires a good deal of dedication and tenacity and deserves careful planning and attention. Ironically, some people spend more time planning their next vacation or where to go to lunch than they do on planning their careers. You also need to look objectively at your own qualifications, aptitude, and previous experience to see if a particular career would make a reasonable fit. For example, if you majored in English literature, you will not easily attain admission to medical school, with or without great connections, unless you have also taken the proper pre-med requirements.

Self-Disclosure

My husband is the kind of person who can talk to anyone. In the grocery store, he jokes with the cashier; on the bus, he talks to the passenger sitting next to him; on the street, he even talks to little old ladies. His outgoing nature used to drive me nuts. Being more reserved, I once thought condescendingly that I was more dignified than he. Today, I realize his personality is more suited to successful networking. To be most effective at networking, you should feel free to talk to anyone, the Prince of Wales or the local street sweeper.

When I was growing up, my mother told me not to talk to strangers. For many cautious parents, this, of course, is still sound advice to give your children. But that warning has to be tempered with the need to reach out and interact with others. You cannot keep your kids in protective cocoons all their lives; even if that were possible, in doing so, you would substantially limit the many positive social transactions that could come from talking to strangers or remote acquaintances.

To be successful at networking, you must be able to disclose who you are, what you've done, and what you want or need. Toot your horn a little. That's the only way people can assess your value to them and help you get what you want. In return, listen to others and try to help them get what they need. Let me cite an example. Deirdre is a consummate networker with a friendly, self-disclosing personality. A free-spirited and gregarious person, she has traveled around the world and worked as a private investigator, sales representative, and product promoter. At a holiday party, she was chatting with another guest, the president of a human resources recruiting firm. Impressed by Deirdre's sincerity and enthusiasm, she asked Deirdre for an interview the following week. "I didn't even know I was being interviewed at the party! If anything, I might have said some things that wouldn't have been appropriate," says Deirdre. The next week, she was offered a job as a recruiter. In this case, Deirdre's ability to share her ideas in a social situation yielded immediate success.

Here is another real-life example of how a self-disclosing conversation led not only to a job, but also to a major career change. Joy was a sales representative for a conference center, but she was beginning to feel that it was not the right career for her. She had attained considerable experience in writing and editing before moving on to her sales career, and she was thinking of leaving her present career to return to writing, but she did not know exactly how to make the switch.

One day, she was making a sales presentation to a manager at an international pharmaceutical firm, and she began to make small talk. Joy noticed a plaque on the manager's wall. With the confidence of a seasoned salesperson, she engaged the manager in a conversation about how he had been awarded the plaque. The manager talked about his background and politely asked Joy about hers. Joy told him that she had once worked as a writer and editor for a textbook publishing firm. The manager asked Joy many questions about her experience and later told her that this company had some openings in its medical publications area. Would she please send him a sample of her writing?

By being friendly and curious, Joy learned more about the manager and found out what his company needed. That's how she was able to find her present job as a medical writer. She recognized an opportunity to sell some of her skills at what otherwise would not be considered a "job interview."

Altruism and Empowerment

Networking has been called a two-way street, but it is better described as a multi-dimensional system. You cannot help someone one day and expect to call in the chit the next day. More likely, you will help a co-worker, and one day your co-worker's friend may give you a hand.

Helping others is an integral part of networking. In every networking situation, one person helps another by doing a favor or by giving the other person an important piece of information about a suitable opportunity. Thus, to be successful at networking, you must be willing to give help as well as to receive help. When you have the opportunity to help someone by giving some helpful advice or a piece of information, do it. By doing so, you plant a seed that could one day bear fruit. The networking system works only because of people's willingness to help one another, to receive as well as to reciprocate.

Networking is synergistic, creating a positive energy greater than the sum of each of the network's individual links. Acting together, each link supports and reinforces the needs and goals of the other links. These linkages are so efficient that psychologist Stanley Milgram theorized that anyone could reach anyone by connecting with people in their extended networks. In *Psychology Today,* Milgram described how he asked a sample of people in Massachusetts to use their contacts to reach a randomly selected group in Nebraska. Milgram's sample was able to contact the randomly chosen people in Nebraska within two links.

Through reaching and helping others on an individual basis or through a community group, you will not only feel good about yourself for doing a good deed, but you will also expose yourself to networking opportunities. One day you may have the fortune of benefiting from a community contact. Many aspiring networkers volunteer for community service, such as the Big Brothers/Big Sisters program, the Lions' Club, or a literacy project. They gain the joy of helping others as well as the benefit of making valuable contacts. Large corporate charities like the United Way are well known for giving ambitious corporate citizens the visibility and leadership skills that catapult them to higher positions.

Serving others has another advantage: namely, building your self-esteem. A former boss of mine once explained that when someone asks for a favor and you do the favor, you suddenly elevate that person in your mind. After all, you wouldn't do favors for someone you thought poorly of, would you? Even though you are doing the favor, you end up thinking more highly of the person seeking your help.

Perhaps it boils down to an even simpler equation: people like to be needed and looked up to. When someone asks you for a favor or for advice, that person is looking up to you. By bestowing the favor, you feel good about yourself, you feel important, you feel empowered, and you feel needed.

Making Opportunity

Networking is about helping others and asking others for help. When you ask for their help, you empower them, and when they ask for your help, you feel empowered. "The vertical to horizontal power shift that networks bring about will be enormously liberating for individuals. Hierarchies promote moving up and getting ahead, producing stress, tension, and anxiety. Networking empowers the individual, and people in networks tend to nurture one another," writes *Megatrends* author John Naisbitt,

If you feel depressed and apathetic, networking gives you ways to improve your situation. Because you have techniques that can help get you out of the rut, you do not need to feel stuck. In their highly acclaimed book *The One Minute Manager,* Kenneth Blanchard and Spencer Johnson advise us to take a minute out of our day to look into the faces of the people we manage, and realize that they are our most important resource. But you do not need to be a manager to take advantage of this wisdom. Look into the faces of the people around you. By communicating and sharing your ideas and objectives with them, you make them your best resources.

Connections with other people — seeking their help or encouragement or giving it in return — allow you to grow in your profession without fear or embarrassment. Adele Scheele notes: "The fact is that we are dependent on each other. It's just that simple, and too often we refuse to acknowledge it."

Gratitude

The cardinal sin of networking is forgetting to recognize the networking help you receive. Because networking is based on helping one another, it is critical that you acknowledge when someone has helped you. An old proverb states: "When you drink from the spring, remember the source." The best way to show your thanks is by acknowledging and remembering the people who help you. If possible, try to think of some way you can return the favor by sharing your own special skill or some useful information.

Kirk, a manager in his fifties at a large corporation, is now starting his own business with his wife, Trish. Kirk feels the salary he makes working for his present company will not cover new expenses such as sending his children to private East Coast colleges. Kirk and Trish have used networking to build their clientele. Says Kirk, "The neat thing about the world of favors is that a favor usually costs relatively little to the person giving, but can be of great value to the person getting the favor. For example, an attorney friend of ours wrote a letter for us to help solve a legal dispute. It was a 'nit' to him, but it saved us tremendous time. Later, I was able to help him with some computer issues that were a piece of cake for me, but were a huge puzzle to him."

If you cannot return the favor, you can show your appreciation through a short letter, a special phone call, or a modest gift. These simple gestures show your gratitude for the information that helped you reach a particular goal.

Saying thanks is common courtesy, and good manners are essential in business and social affairs, but the number of people who have forgotten common courtesy could dismay you. If you give wedding, birthday, or graduation gifts to your relatives or friends, you expect a note of thanks. I finally told one lazy nephew not to expect a birthday gift until I received a thank-you note for his Christmas gift!

While networking information is not as tangible as a $50 savings bond, it is no less valuable. In a society that depends on information to function effectively, a single clue can make the difference in solving the mysteries of getting a promotion or starting a new enterprise.

Send thank-you letters and make thank-you calls to those who help you. By doing so, you reinforce personal contacts and will be better remembered. Showing your gratitude is especially important because so many people fail to acknowledge the help they receive.

When I was looking for a technical writing job in Silicon Valley, an acquaintance gave me the name of a well-regarded consultant in the communications training field. I called Susan, and she told me that a former student of hers was looking for a technical writer. I called him and interviewed for the job. After getting the interview, I wrote Susan the following thank-you note:

> Dear Susan,
>
> Thanks for your helpful advice about getting jobs in Santa Clara. I called your former student, Tom, at Storage Technology Corporation and got an interview for a job. I'm very excited about working for his company.
>
> Thank you again for your help. I will let you know the results of my interview.
>
> Sincerely,
> Cynthia Chin-Lee

In addition to sending her the note, a few months later I took Susan out to dinner; I also invited the acquaintance who had given me Susan's name.

You could dismiss this thank-you business as a mere formality without much consequence, but I know from experience that it pays off. For example, Susan became an informal mentor, always available to me when I sought career and personal advice. She also introduced me to a woman who was influential in my being hired for a challenging and highly visible training contract with AT&T.

If you fail to thank someone, the results can be harsh. In the children's fairy tale, "Sleeping Beauty," the fairy who was left off the guest list for the princess's party cast a spell on the kingdom. While you might not be doomed to sleep for a hundred years by slighting someone who helps you, you probably will not be helped again.

Persistence

After you thank the people who help you, keep in regular contact — even if that means only an annual birthday card or Christmas letter — to solidify your contacts and transform your casual acquaintances into allies, mentors, and friends. When you read an article relevant to your contact's interests, clip it and send it to her. When you get a piece of information that can help your brother-in-law in looking for a job in Portland, give him a call. The key here is not just to call when you need something; networking means socializing, playing tennis with the boss, and lunching with friends even when there's no specific objective in mind. As much as you can, be a real friend, not a networking barracuda.

The famous inventor Thomas Edison said, "Genius is one percent inspiration and ninety-nine percent perspiration." Like anything worthwhile, networking takes one percent of inspiration, but also requires a good deal of perspiration and persistence. Despite the effort involved, pursuing a contact persistently and politely often pays multifold dividends.

A high school friend, Carolyn, was a television reporter for eight years with little hope of ever becoming an anchor. She decided she needed a change, so she examined related fields such as public relations and government. She consulted with another former reporter who was serving as press aide to the mayor of Jacksonville, Florida. That press aide told Carolyn that a job was being created for which Carolyn might qualify. Carolyn contacted the division chief, a person she had worked with previously as a reporter. The division chief told her it would be a while before the position was open, but she would keep Carolyn in mind for it.

Carolyn called her every month for a year and kept track of the listing of city openings because the position was a government job. Carolyn says: "When the job was finally open, I had to apply like everyone else and go through the civil service examination procedure. There were 400 applicants for the job and, while the division chief was interested in me, she could choose only from the names on the qualification list. I almost missed out because I had recently married and was using a name that the division chief did not recognize. But because I was calling every month, it was easy to clear the mix-up over my name and she called me in for an interview." Because of the combination of her persistence and personal contact, Carolyn got the job as Information Services Coordinator of Jacksonville.

The Power of Personal Contact

Because of mass communication, global travel, and the instantaneous transfer of images and words, people have amazing choices in careers, lifestyles, and consumer products, many more choices than they had years ago. For example, an employer might receive thousands of résumés just by advertising a position in a national newspaper. How does the employer make a decision after skimming the hundreds of résumés that invade the office in the daily mail? The employer often depends on personal contacts to get information about the applicants or to refer applicants directly.

Likewise, with all the options available, how do you decide on a particular career or job? According to the *Mother's Almanac*, a guidebook for raising children, there are more than 300,000 possible careers. How can you prepare yourself to face 300,000 options? By exposing yourself to personal contacts in many different fields, you can begin to find the career choices most suitable for you. Informational interviewing, discussed in Chapter Four, is an excellent way for you to discover appropriate jobs or work environments.

When you apply for a job, it's difficult to make your résumé stand out in a stack of 500 other résumés. Instead of using gimmicks to get attention from the prospective employer, use your network. Specifically, if you know of a position that you really want, find a personal contact, such as a current employee of the company, preferably one who knows the hiring manager. If the target company is fairly large, you can usually find a current employee of the company by asking people you know (your friend's friend, a neighbor's relative, a fellow graduate of your alma mater). If you are selected to interview for the job, by mentioning the acquaintance you elevate your chances considerably. And if your personal contact is a senior ranking officer of the company, your chances of being hired often increase enormously.

The problem of the abundance of options afflicts the consumer market as well. When you go down the aisle of your friendly, neighborhood market, owned by a gigantic, multinational conglomerate, how do you choose which toilet tissue to buy? There might be a dozen different brands. You might pick the one you saw advertised on television umpteen times or you might choose the brand your mom used. Manufacturers know that too many choices confuse people. Thus, some of them take the media route, spending a prince's ransom for television, radio, and print ads. Others sell over the phone, through the mail, or through the most direct route, door-to-door salespeople.

Like many others, I cannot resist a kid selling raffle tickets for school, a Girl Scout selling cookies, or a friend selling Amway. Because personal contact is immediate and compelling, it makes it hard to say "no." While I can throw away a letter from yet another charity begging for my hard-earned dollar, I will not say no to a friend who wants a pledge for an AIDS walkathon. Transfer this principle to the manager in search of an employee or a person in search of a job. If you make a favorable impression on a manager through any number of possible networking routes, and you more or less fill the job qualifications, you will probably get hired. Thus, it seems, the more high tech society becomes, the more we crave a personal touch.

My friend Nancy, a young professional with lots of energy and ambition, wanted to teach in her field of expertise at the local community college. Although no jobs were currently advertised as open, Nancy began making contacts with the program coordinator at the college. She volunteered to be the liaison between the college program and the local professional organization and set up a dinner meeting that focused on education in the profession. Both the college administration and the professional organization began to know Nancy as a "doer." Through her initiative, she was able to develop a trusted relationship with the program coordinator.

Nancy also befriended an instructor in the program who was in a position that Nancy wanted; that instructor worked full-time in the field and taught part-time in the evening. Nancy discussed with the instructor her interest in teaching part-time. To Nancy's delight, the instructor encouraged her and asked Nancy to be a guest speaker in her class that semester.

Nancy prepared her lecture carefully and was able to show her ability to teach and lead a class. When she applied to become a part-time instructor, she was able to supply a recommendation from her friend, the current faculty member, who had seen her teach. She had also already established a positive relationship with the program coordinator. Nancy left little to chance in order to get the teaching position she desired.

Despite strong competition for the part-time teaching positions, Nancy was the top candidate and was hired as an instructor. Her networking strategy worked.

In Summary

Make opportunities for yourself by developing a positive "networking state of mind." You can cultivate this attitude by being open and alert to opportunities, setting goals, and becoming more self-disclosing. Learn to share your accomplishments and abilities, and don't be shy about seeking what you need from others.

Because networking is a give and take endeavor, be generous to others with information, advice, and encouragement. In return for your altruism and volunteering spirit, your self-esteem and confidence will grow, making you more self-empowered. As good things begin to happen, remember to acknowledge and thank the people who help and encourage you. Show your gratitude without hesitation. By sharing your success with others, you will gain even greater success. Communicate frequently with your contacts, even if you call them only briefly on the phone or write them a short note.

Finally, pursue your objectives persistently using traditional methods as well as networking. Building a personal network takes a special combination of ingredients, including diligence, openness, creativity, and communication skills.

The fine art of networking requires extra effort and follow-through. Yet in our highly competitive world, it can be the critical edge that sets you apart from the rest. The bottom line is that cultivating the right contacts can help get what you want out of your life.

3

Sources for Networking

A stranger is just a friend you haven't met yet.
Girl Scout saying

In this chapter, you will learn how to identify your existing network and how to expand it. You scoff, "But I don't have a network!" Few of us live so remotely that we do not already have at least a minimal network. The typical adult makes between 500 to 1,000 social acquaintances in a lifetime. Most of us come into contact with thousands of people a year: the mail delivery person, the clerk at the grocery store, your medical doctor, your business associates, your manager, your sister from Denver, a new person at church, a neighbor down the block, the wife of a co-worker at the company picnic, your high school buddy. What you may not realize is that each of these individuals could be a valuable contact who will introduce you to his or her contacts.

Your network may not include the President of the United States, members of the old boy network, or famous

Hollywood directors, but the lack of these does not make your network any less powerful. In fact, contacts with famous or fabulously wealthy people, while nice to have, will not necessarily give you the desired result. An exception to this rule might be people in public service, your congressional representatives, city council, or locally elected officials, who depend on your vote for attaining and keeping their jobs. These kinds of public servants, active or retired, often have extensive networks that you can tap into. Many congressional representatives employ a professional ombudsman or troubleshooter who can solve problems for you.

Think Globally and Act Locally

Of course, you do not need to start making contacts at the top; start small and grow according to your own dreams. To borrow a phrase from the environmental movement: think globally and act locally. Think in global terms about the kinds of contacts you would like to have. Brainstorm with your friends and family members about potential contacts. Then start making contacts locally, with your own close friends, family, and business associates. Make contacts close to home and let those contacts branch outward to better and more effective contacts. *Megatrends* author John Naisbitt describes the new trend in networking as "both ubiquitous and essential. The Old Boy Network is elitist; the new network is egalitarian."

Marianna, a quality program manager, used networking and informational interviewing after she graduated with a master's degree at a university in Indiana. Knowing that she wanted to return to her native California, she called and wrote many friends, family, and professors who may have contacts in the Bay Area. She says,

"My strategy worked. I called everyone I knew who might have a remote connection to a company in California. Actually, it took me longer than I expected, eight months, to find the kind of job I wanted. But, of course, I'm very happy with the results."

A friend, Lisa, explains another type of networking that occurred while she was job hunting:

"I took my computer to the computer repair shop. I told the repair person that I was a writer looking for a job. The shop is owned by a Dow Jones company. The repair woman told me that Dow Jones owns a major newspaper so she told me to try applying for a job. When I hesitated, she brought out a 100-page listing of the job openings available at Dow Jones companies. I call that synchronicity. Can you imagine the possibility of finding a job through a computer repair shop?"

As Lisa's example shows, casual acquaintances and strangers often provide the best contacts. Learn from the millionaires. Professor Thomas Stanley, a Georgia State University marketing professor, has held discussion groups with millionaires across the country. He reports, "Aside from lots of money, what do most millionaires have in common? A very big Rolodex. Networking ability may be the key to their success.... They'll start making deals with strangers in the room."

Although it may seem counter to common sense, casual acquaintances and strangers can be better contacts than close friends and relatives. Mark Granovetter, Harvard researcher and author of *Getting Jobs: A Study of Contacts and Careers,* found that people who found jobs through contacts are more likely to find jobs through a weak contact, someone they did not know very well, rather than a strong contact, such as a family member or close friend. You are more likely to find a job through information from a casual acquaintance than from an old crony.

In his research, Granovetter measured the strength of a contact by the number of times that the two people had met. He defined three categories of contacts: those who met at least twice a week (often), more than once a year but less than twice a week (occasionally), and once a year or less (rarely). Here are his findings:

> Of those in the interview sample who found their job through contacts, 16.7 percent reported that they were seeing their contact "often," 55.6 percent "occasionally," while 27.8 percent saw him "rarely." The skew is to the weak side of the continuum. Moreover, those who found their job through weaker ties reported much more often that their contacts "put in a good word" for them, as well as telling them about the job.

Granovetter speculates that good friends may be reluctant to pass on job information because of the inherent risk to the relationship. Casual acquaintances, however, have little to lose when they refer you to a job. Therefore, when you consider the contacts that you need to reach your objective, do not limit them to your close associates. In fact, you must go beyond intimate friends and family to get the appropriate contact.

A casual acquaintance can also be a better contact because he or she might not stereotype you in your present profession. For instance, if you are a housewife, your own family and close friends may have a difficult time thinking of you as a high-flying sales representative. However, an acquaintance, who does not see you washing dirty dishes every day, can visualize you more easily in a new role.

Thus, your acquaintance may more readily conclude how your contacts in the community, organizational skills, and initiative would help make you an effective salesperson. In addition, those close to you often have a vested interest in seeing that you do not change. Who will cook their dinner and do their laundry if you become a successful sales executive?

Casual contacts who provide a significant piece of information to you can later become your friends. After landing a job because of a contact's information, make a point of getting to know your contact better. Recognize the generosity and thoughtfulness of the contact who made your goal possible. In many cases, you can transform those initially weak but valuable contacts into closer relationships and friendships.

Building the Network

The five steps to building your personal network are as follows:
1. Identify your existing network.
2. Expand your network through contacting your existing network.
3. Join organizations and be an active participant.
4. Collect business cards.
5. Learn to introduce yourself to strangers.

If you master these steps, your network can become a powerful force that generates opportunities and challenges to invigorate and brighten your future.

1. Identify Your Existing Network

Start by making a list of people who are close to you. Include family, friends, co-workers, people who owe you a favor, people to whom you owe a favor, store or service personnel, even your Avon lady. Even if you have a specific goal in mind, such as getting a job in medical research, do not limit your list to logically related people. For instance, if your sister-in-law is an attorney, your first impulse may be to exclude her as a possible source of contacts in your field. However, you may find out later that her college roommate is a lab director at the National Institutes of Health. You will find it to your advantage to tell everyone you know about your goal to become a medical researcher.

This book is another example of why you should not limit your network to logically related contacts. I wanted to write this book for several years, but never seriously pursued a publisher. While on a business trip, my brother-in-law, Phil, who lives in another state, went to visit his high school buddy, Rand, a publisher's representative and writer. On that same trip, he saw me. Knowing that I write freelance articles, my brother-in-law gave me Rand's card, in case we would have some common interests.

A few weeks later, I called Rand, and told him about my book idea. He asked me to send him a proposal. After reading it, he contacted Slawson Communications, who published the first edition of this book.

Networking is responsible for taking the idea for this book from a daydream to a reality, yet I may have made these contacts earlier had I asked my brother-in-law about his contacts in publishing. Because Phil is a human resources manager for a computer company, I never imagined that he could help me in this venture.

Roger von Oech, creativity researcher and author of *A Kick in the Seat of the Pants and A Whack on the Side of the Head,* advises that we suspend judgment of ideas in the germinal stages of creative thinking. Look at the big picture. Think of people in whole terms, not just as the role that they play in relationship to you. Thus, when you are trying to get acting jobs, don't forget to tell your brother who is a math teacher; he may have a fraternity brother who works in Hollywood.

Von Oech says that many ideas that you may initially drop because of their improbable nature could be the stepping stones to a brilliant idea. Likewise in networking, people you may think have no contacts in your field of interest could come up with several good contacts from their personal associations.

In identifying your existing network, examine these categories of people as a starting point:
- Family
- Friends
- Educational associates
- Business associates
- Social acquaintances
- Neighbors
- Professional advisers

Family

In his research, Mark Granovetter found that younger, less experienced workers tend to use family and friends as a primary source of job information. Older, more experienced workers, on the other hand, are more likely to use business associates as sources of contacts. The exception to this rule is an older, experienced person who is changing careers. In that case, experienced or inexperienced, a person should consult family members. If you are making a career change, your family contacts will be important. Family members often work in diverse industries and have contacts in the industries that you need to make a career move.

For instance, I come from a large family of five children. In my immediate family, including my parents, siblings, and their spouses, we have two doctors, a banker, a couple of homemakers, a writer, an engineer, a computer programmer, an office manager, a human resources manager, and an artist. Think of the variety of contacts you can generate within your own family.

A recent college graduate, Catherine, tried using the on-campus interviewing program at her university but quickly realized that she was not getting anywhere. Catherine had good grades, but she really had no clear direction on how and where to look for her first job.

Catherine's older sister offered to submit her résumé to the company where she worked. Catherine told me how she used her family contact to get a job:

> When my sister asked for my résumé to submit to her company's summer hire program, I wasn't sure which area really held the most interest for me. We solved this problem by mentioning many areas within the company in my cover letter. I didn't expect to receive the results that I did. I was phoned at school a few weeks before graduation by a manager in customer support, who interviewed me over the phone, and offered a three-month position in her department. I will definitely feel more confident about speaking up to the people I know, my family or friends, when I'm ready to do my next job hunt.

Some people hesitate to use family members as sources of information, because they consider that asking for help from relatives smacks of nepotism. This is especially true if their relatives are famous celebrities or multimillionaires. Frankly, most of us do not have this problem. If you feel this way, think of your situation in another light: you could get your first job because your father is Walter Cronkite, but doing your job well and retaining it for the long term depends on your performance.

Developing contacts through family members should be a natural extension of daily conversations with your immediate family or the less frequent visits, phone calls, or letters to your extended family. Follow the advice of Ma Bell, and "reach out and touch someone." Use the phone as an important networking tool, good for keeping in touch, exchanging ideas, and making contacts. The President of the United States, for example, uses the phone extensively to keep in close contact with national and world leaders.

While your family members sometimes have a vested interest in seeing you stay the same, they also have a vested interest in helping you. (If you fail to get a job, they may have to support you.) By sharing your goals and aspirations with your family members, you will find it easier to share them with people less close to you. In other words, even if you think your family members would not be able to generate any helpful contacts, tell them about your goals. By talking about your plans, you will have practiced expressing some complex ideas, feelings, or concepts. Family and friends can help clarify your goals and objectives; then, when you converse with an acquaintance or a stranger, you will sound clearer and more articulate.

However, some family members could have a stronger interest in making sure you do not change; they may be afraid that you will abandon them if you are successful. You may be typecast by your family as Cousin Jennifer or Grandpa Bob, not as the executive, artist, or entrepreneur that you are striving to be. We are all susceptible to lowering our expectations of ourselves and diminishing our ambitions if everyone around us expects us to flop. If this is your case, keep your goals mum at home, but try to surround yourself with positive people in other aspects of your life.

Here is a sheet for you to record your family contacts. (Note: all the forms in this book can be reproduced at 120 percent to fit on standard paper.)

Remember to include your extended relatives; they often can be better sources of contacts than your closer family members. Although you do not need an excuse to call a long lost cousin, networking may even help you strengthen precious family bonds.

Friends

Like your family members, friends can generate many contacts for you. They often have contacts in a large number of fields at many different companies. Because friends are generally in your age range, they can offer information appropriate for your career stage, whether that is totally inexperienced or chief executive officer level. If you are geographically mobile, your friends can have better information than family members who have lived in the same town for generations.

My former co-worker, Peter, is a bright, articulate engineer and businessman, with mechanical engineering degrees from two highly rated, competitive schools. Tall and attractive, he commands attention and seems to have everything required to be successful.

Family

Name	Address	Phone	E-mail	Comments

Peter had worked as a product engineer for a few years at a medium-sized firm, with the ambition to be promoted to a more glamorous marketing position. Despite his efforts to be noticed, no promotion seemed forthcoming, and he felt stuck. Peter describes how networking with a friend helped him get his first product marketing job:

> I became disenchanted with my position when it no longer appeared there would be opportunities in marketing within the coming year. As soon as this became obvious, I started looking for a new position. I immediately phoned two contacts, one an ex-manager of my current company, and the other a friend of my wife's.
>
> Although my wife's friend did not know of any specific positions, she knew that a couple of managers in her group were starting to look for a new employee. She gave my résumé to these people, and I received a phone call about a month later. The call was a complete surprise, but it eventually led to a job offer.

Peter had a definite aim in mind and went after it. Through networking with friends, he eventually was able to get a coveted marketing position. Usually, networking is deliberate, but occasionally it happens before you even realize it, such as when a friend introduces you in a new social setting. My friend Lisa stumbled into a networking opportunity when she was living in Hong Kong:

> A friend in banking called me up to ask if by chance I knew anything about launching a satellite in China. As a matter of fact, I shared an interest in the Chinese satellite launches with my father and kept a file on the subject. The friend asked me to send him the file. Later that week, my friend asked me to go to dinner with him. He told me nothing about the dinner party, but he said I wouldn't be

Friends

Name	Address	Phone	E-mail	Comments

disappointed. We walked into a dinner meeting in a penthouse suite overlooking the Hong Kong harbor; a group of men dressed in business suits were sitting around the table. They turned out to be satellite lawyers, insurers, and promoters.

Dinner conversation went quickly to business, and with my knowledge of Chinese satellite launches, I was able to correct an Englishman who had inaccurately quoted the number of Chinese launches. It was my entrance into the group. Within two weeks, I was assistant to the chairman of the company that initiated one of the first launches of an American satellite on Chinese rockets. This was my best success with networking — not manipulating people, but knowing that possibilities exist everywhere.

As these examples show, sometimes you consult your friends intentionally to get help. At other times, your social interactions with friends will unknowingly lead to new opportunities. Note that in Lisa's case, she was open minded about new possibilities, and she was willing to be self-disclosing and take some risks in order to participate in conversations with strangers.

Use the form to enter the names of the friends in your personal network.

Educational Associates

Your educational associates come from a gamut of schools, from kindergarten to university. Even after you graduate from a formal college or a graduate program, you can continue making contacts by attending classes at vocational schools, community colleges, and university extension schools. Ideally, you will build close relationships with your instructor and classmates. Your contacts are not limited to the classroom, however, because most of these educational institutions also have career advisers, job centers, and alumni networks.

Instructors or Professors

Your teachers may serve as primary contacts, especially for jobs in their areas of expertise. If you performed well in their classes, share your goals with your instructors. Instructors often have a wealth of contacts in industry, including their former students and their fellow professors, and through their own work in industry (many teachers consult on the side). If you are planning to stay in your instructor's field of study, ask if he or she is willing to hire you as an assistant.

Most instructors and professors have an altruistic attitude that led them to choose teaching as a career. Thus, they are often willing to take the time to help. Here is the story of one of my former students. In her late thirties, Jaci wanted a change from her job as a production control manager for a manufacturing firm. She quit her job, moved to the mountains, and became an independent contractor hanging wallpaper professionally. Still not satisfied, and needing a better income, she did some soul searching and decided to enter the growing technical writing field.

Jaci enrolled in my technical writing class even though she lived 100 miles away in the Sierra foothills. She made the weekly trek to my evening class, often with her husband in tow. She explains how she got her first job in technical writing through networking:

> I had never been a real believer in networking until I tried it. In my first attempt, I was able to completely change careers and land a job at a major Fortune 500 company without a reduction in salary.

I had decided to change my career and started taking certificate classes at the local college. The teacher arranged several guest lecturers as part of the class to give us a view into the various jobs relating to the field. One lecture was about a type of work that was similar to my work in production control. After the lecture was finished, I talked to the guest speaker and told her that I was interested in this field of work. I also handed her my business card. The next afternoon she called me for an interview, and the rest is history. I am now working as a publications editor in charge of a major new project in my department.

Classmates

Many times, you will make bonds more easily with classmates than with an instructor because you are on the same level. Additionally, you share a common experience with your classmates: assignments, exams, lectures, and grades. In an ideal teaching environment, you learn as much or more from your peers as you do from your professor.

Carolyn attended George Washington University and graduated with a degree in broadcast communications. She wanted to enter the television news field, an extremely competitive market. To get started, she consulted her professor, who gave her the name of a television station in Virginia that had hired one of her students earlier. Carolyn was able to get her first job in Virginia, and a subsequent job in a larger market through her connection to her professor's student:

> I was a teaching assistant at George Washington University and nearing graduation. My college professor suggested that I investigate a television station in Harrisonburg, Virginia, that had provided a job for another one of her

students. And as it turned out, they hired me as a reporter as soon as the position was open, primarily because of the reputation of the other student. He had worked out very well for them.

He eventually moved to a job in Jacksonville, Florida; I contacted him at my professor's recommendation. He said, "There's a job open here now; why don't you apply for it?" I applied and they hired me as a reporter and a talk show host. I had never even met him; I had only called to tell him that I followed in his footsteps.

Career or Job Placement Centers

In addition to teachers and classmates, you can take advantage of career or job placement centers as a source of contacts. Many high schools, vocational schools, colleges, and universities have special career placement centers to help students find jobs and get career counseling. If you are still a student, or live near the campus, you can take advantage of the resources of the placement center. Most colleges and universities allow current students and alumni to use the resources of the campus placement center. And while most placement centers do not advertise their resources to the general community, they sometimes do not restrict access to students or graduates only. In addition to placement centers that are part of a college or university, many communities have career centers open to the general public for a nominal fee.

Placement centers often set up interviews with representatives of local and national companies in various fields. They usually keep binders of information on local and national companies that you can use to research specific careers and companies. They also run workshops on specific job-hunting skills, such as résumé writing, interviewing skills, and goal-setting.

Of special interest for the new job-hunter are internships, cooperative programs, and externships. The placement center often provides a service to match students or recent graduates to an appropriate internship, cooperative, or externship. Your field of study may also offer an internship program that gives you college credit for getting work experience in business or industry.

The internship can provide a paying or volunteer job at a local company or non-profit organization. It can last a few weeks, the summer, or a college semester. Usually, the intern works with one or two staff members to learn how to participate in and contribute to meaningful aspects of the job as well as to do some clerical chores.

The cooperative, or co-op, is similar to the internship, but usually lasts a longer time, such as working full-time or part-time for a semester or year. Normally, college co-ops are paid positions.

A former intern at a Fortune 500 company, Stacy recounts how she broke into the editing field. Knowing how difficult it is to get hired without any experience, Stacy accepted a volunteer internship so that she could gain experience and make contacts:

> I was in my second year of college as an English major at Sacramento State University. By chance, through a professional association, I found an internship. A local company was interested in finding an intern for one of its writing groups. I really had no experience to offer them, but then they couldn't afford to pay me. It was a great trade-off: my time and effort for exposure to the area of technical communications.
>
> During that internship, I learned their process of technical writing, met several people from different areas in the company and learned what kinds of careers existed

in technical communications. When the internship ended, I decided to pursue a career in technical writing.

The following summer, one of the people I worked with as an intern recommended me as production editor for another group at the same company. I worked there as an intern and later as a full-time contractor for a year. Next I got a full-time permanent position as an editor for yet another group in the same company.

The externship allows you to follow a professional for a few days or a week. You simply shadow the person as he or she does the work. Although there is no participation, you learn how the person spends time, and what kinds of activities and people are involved. Externships do not pay, but they provide a rare opportunity to get an inside look at a particular career or company. Some schools sponsor programs to match you with an externship over the semester break, or the winter or spring holiday.

On a one-to-one basis, advisers or career counselors at these job placement centers often can review your résumé or help you practice interviewing skills. The advisers or staff of the placement center are a good source of potential contacts.

In contrast to the career-oriented counseling you receive, at the same placement center you can usually find information about part-time or full-time jobs that are less glamorous, such as gardening, house-cleaning, or secretarial. Sometimes the placement center has two sections: one with career-oriented opportunities, and the other with clerical and manual labor jobs. Many people use these clerical or manual jobs to support themselves while they attend school and to generate contacts in the community. Your career might begin by sweeping floors for an industrial company, but that does not mean your career will end there. For example, one of my mentors immigrated to the United States as a teenager. He started his career as a houseboy for a family so he could earn money to support himself through school. His experience with an American family facilitated his assimilation to American culture, exposing him to the ways of his adopted country. Now he is president of an engineering firm that has three offices and more than fifty employees.

College Advisers and Alumni

Placement centers often have career advisers and lists of alumni who are willing to grant informational interviews to those who seek information about a field. Talk to the career advisers and make an appointment with them to get the individual attention you require.

If you attended a large school or a school with particularly loyal alumni, you may have an active alumni club in your city. Most college graduates begin receiving the alumni magazine and solicitations to join alumni club activities immediately after graduation. Alumni clubs often have a formal program in which they solicit alumni to volunteer as informal career advisers. Such volunteers are the ideal candidates to call for an interview; you don't have to prove yourself to them because you have already proven yourself by having attended the same college. You can also make some excellent contacts with other alumni through the club activities.

Use the form to record the names of your teachers, classmates, and alumni advisers.

Educational Associates

Name	Address	Phone	E-mail	Comments

Business Associates

Business associates, including current or former co-workers, managers, or subordinates, provide a major source of contacts for people with many years of experience in their field. In addition to the people you work with directly, people who work in other divisions of the company could prove to be worthwhile contacts for you. Many large companies sponsor clubs and events where you can network within the company. Take advantage of these opportunities. The people you meet at the company picnic, the department softball team, karate club, or Toastmasters club may be excellent sources of information that can help get your next job or promotion.

Current or Former Co-workers

Current or former co-workers offer a significant source of contacts because they know you and your work. Also, because co-workers transfer jobs and companies frequently, they are a key way to learn about new positions within a company or the industry. Co-workers, thus, have an important advantage over family members or friends: their contacts are likely to be appropriate for your current experience. On the other hand, if you are trying to make a career switch, co-workers may not serve as appropriate contacts because they can typecast you in a role that you are trying to overcome.

Many people have been able to find new jobs through staying in contact with previous co-workers. For example, Linda was a former teacher, who worked as a junior editor. Her company was suffering from aggressive overseas competition and laid her off after a few months. Linda knew an engineer who left the company before the major layoff occurred. She had edited a sales brochure for the product he was working on, so he had first-hand knowledge of her abilities. When Linda was laid off by the company, she called the engineer, who now worked at a different company, about editing positions. He was able to recommend her to his new company, where she was quickly placed in a similar position.

Current or Former Bosses

Like co-workers, current or former bosses often can help you find a new position. Your present manager may not want you to leave because replacing you would be difficult. Use discretion when dealing with a manager who could oppose your leaving to seek better opportunities.

Former managers can help you with a new job by hiring you directly or providing information about jobs at their company or within the industry. Most managers have a wide range of contacts and responsibilities and can be more aware of what is happening in the company and the industry than a peer. If a manager leaves to go to another company, you may be asked to join the new staff.

As long as a good working relationship is maintained with the manager, you may find new and better jobs through that relationship. As a technical writer, I have worked for one engineering manager at three different companies, progressing up the corporate ladder as he progressed. I first worked for Tom as an employee in a start-up company. A few years later, he was a vice president at another company, and I was a technical writing consultant. Tom hired me to do consulting work at this company. Later he became president and founder of his own company, and he again hired me, this time to establish the technical publications department.

If you have been working for a few years, keep track of your professional associates, managers, peers, and subordinates. If they are transferred or leave the company to go to another firm, be sure to get their forwarding address and phone number. When they are promoted, attend their promotion parties. If they transfer or leave the company, attend the farewell luncheon. If no one has organized a good-bye party, volunteer.

Be certain that your co-workers know your career aspirations and that you know theirs. When openings occur at their new company, they can keep you informed and refer you to a better opportunity. Likewise, if an opening occurs at your company that is appropriate, you can refer them to the position.

Guy, a computer programmer, found a new job through a referral from his own boss, with whom he had established a candid relationship. His manager, Mark, received a phone call from a recruiter. Although Mark was not interested in the position, he knew Guy was not satisfied with their current company and passed the telephone call to him. Says Guy:

> Mark handed me the phone and I chatted with the recruiter. I had already done an information-gathering interview at the firm with someone who I served with on an industry standards committee. I knew that it was a bright, new company with an organizational structure that made sense for my career goals. The recruiter set up a real interview and asked me to send him my résumé. By the time he received it in the mail, I had already been to the firm for the interview and shortly thereafter had a job offer.

Business Associates

Name	Address	Phone	E-mail	Comments

Current or Former Subordinates or Support Staff

While we do not need to be reminded to be considerate of our peers and bosses, we can easily overlook our subordinates. Such negligence could be costly, especially if your subordinate receives a promotion within your company or another company and ends up as your manager. Be especially courteous to secretaries and administrators. You want them on your side because they are the gatekeepers to information and to the people you want to approach.

Remember to be considerate to everyone, regardless of corporate rank. One of the interns who worked with me has been promoted several times in a short time. Her career has evolved rapidly, and she has been able to refer me to consulting opportunities. Watching younger people get promoted can be frustrating, but your envy will not help you accomplish your objectives.

Use the form to record the names of your business associates.

Customers, Vendors and Suppliers

Customers, vendors, and suppliers can provide many profitable contacts. The individuals in these businesses have a special and often critical business relationship with you. In the case of customers, they often have a specialized network in your field. Moreover, like your colleagues, they understand your abilities because they have seen you at work. Businesses with customer or partnership relationships end up "exchanging" employees so often that some firms sign agreements to prohibit active recruitment of the other company's personnel. Vendors and suppliers have a vested interest in favorable treatment because they want

Customers, Vendors and Suppliers

Name	Address	Phone	E-mail	Comments

your business. They are likely to be as helpful as possible in networking requests.

As the president of his own communications consulting firm in Dallas, Joe has been networking for more than twenty years and he knows how important it is to build a solid reputation. He has made special efforts to build a network of personal contacts in Dallas's technical community. He proudly says that his name always comes up when someone is looking for an expert in data communications.

Joe's style of networking is subtle; he never makes a hard sales pitch because it is not necessary. Educated at Yale and the University of Texas, Joe has made a living as an officer in the armed services, an electronics salesman, technical writer, and engineer. He explains how he once made a valuable contact through one of his suppliers, a typesetting and printing company:

> An expert in fiberglass reinforced plastic was looking for a writer to help him write a book in his field. My typesetter gave him my name. I wound up being the editor for this book that is now used in most universities, and I made some good money at it. This networking information can come from very unexpected sources.

Use the form to record the names of your customers, vendors, or suppliers who are possible contacts.

Social Acquaintances

Your church, Kiwanis club, or swim team seem unlikely places to make contacts, but you may be amazed at how much business is conducted at such diverse gatherings. By joining a church, club, or sports team, you are showing

Social Acquaintances

Name	Address	Phone	E-mail	Comments

an important affiliation that is likely to endear you to fellow members.

Jim, a management consultant, explains how he gets contacts through his love for swimming:

> Some of my best contacts have come through competing on an adult swim team. I swim because I love swimming, not to make contacts. But the shared love of athletic challenge forms a basis of respect and friendship that carries over to business activities.

As a self-employed attorney, Harry founded a local chapter of an educational and community service organization. He reports that most of his clients are referred to him by word of mouth through informal networks and through his association with the community service organization that he started. One of his clients shares why he chose Harry as his personal lawyer:

> My wife and I were looking for an attorney to write our will and create a living trust. We contacted some other lawyers through ads in the paper and even attended one of their seminars, but we just felt more comfortable with Harry. We know Harry pretty well through the club and respect him. It only made sense to choose him as our lawyer over strangers whom we didn't know at all.

If you have an ethnic or racial affiliation, keeping in touch with clubs and associations of your heritage can be surprisingly useful. For instance, the first time Helen Bentley ran for congressional representative in the state of Maryland, she was handily defeated. Bentley has central European origins, and after her initial defeat, she decided to seek the help of her fellow Americans of central European heritage. Now a United States congresswoman, Bentley credits her political success to the ethnic groups who supported her candidacy. People find it easier to help those with whom they have something in common, whether that commonality is the same school, race, or religion.

Paula Bernstein, the author of *Family Ties, Corporate Bonds,* says, "Bosses hire people who fit in and that means fit into the office family.... We are all more comfortable around people who look like us, act like us, share our histories, enjoy the same pleasures. Boating nuts hire other boating nuts. Irish hire Irish." Admittedly, this kind of practice can be discriminatory if taken too far, and all of us need to be alert to the problem of hiring only those people who "fit in" a certain way.

However, you can use the affinity of your group to advantage in making contacts, and you can define your "group" in many different and dynamic ways. For example, you may be a member of organizations as diverse as the Veterans of Foreign Wars, the Lions Club, the Black Journalist Association, or the Masters Swimming Club of Poughkeepsie. Your personal contacts through association with any of these groups can yield business partners, clients, or simply good friends.

Use the following form to record the names of your social acquaintances.

Neighbors

The average American family stays in a home for five years or less, so it is not surprising that few of us take the time to get to know our neighbors. If you live in an apartment building or condominium, your neighbors may change even more frequently. With some effort, however, you can get to know your neighbors, and you may find several contacts who can help you find babysitters, local medical or dental referrals, and perhaps even a job. More important than that, knowing your neighbors may save your life in an emergency, such as an illness, flash flood, or tornado. It's much better to know in advance those you can count on in a crisis.

There are a variety of ways to meet your neighbors. The most direct way is to knock on their door and introduce yourself. If this method sounds too direct, you can wait for an opportunity to see your neighbor working in the yard or taking the dog for a walk. When you catch your neighbor outside, introduce yourself and make conversation. You can also meet people at your office who live in your neighborhood. They can introduce you to their friends in the neighborhood so that your neighborly contacts grow steadily.

Of course, kids often find friends in the neighborhood without much prompting. If you have kids, let them be your ambassadors. They can open many doors with just a smile.

I admittedly don't know my neighbors very well and I envy people who can knock on their neighbor's door for a cup of coffee or an egg. Janice is one of those people. She seems to have a knack for meeting people; she has an outgoing personality and is constantly planning social gatherings and trips. She lives in an older, upscale neighborhood with towering, old shade trees and is friendly with most of her neighbors. Her neighborhood even has a local dining club where neighbors eat together at a neighbor's home in groups of eight or ten. At one such dinner, she told one of her neighbors that she was unhappy as a financial analyst in a large, faltering bank and about her wish to move on to a stimulating work environment.

Janice's neighbor owned his own business, a real estate and insurance office with about twenty-five

Neighbors

Name	Address	Phone	E-mail	Comments

employees. He offered her a job at his company in community and public relations. By getting to know her neighbor, Janice not only landed a new job and career, she also ended up carpooling to work with the boss.

Use the form to record the names of your neighbors.

Professional Advisers

Your personal professional advisers, such as your family doctor, dentist, accountant, or lawyer, can also be sources of contacts. You would not question the propriety of asking your family doctor for a recommendation for a medical specialist, but consider that your doctor could also help with contacts useful in other situations, such as looking for a job, a babysitter, or a home to rent. Like your vendors and suppliers, your personal advisers should be considerate and helpful because they appreciate your business.

Allison is a recent college graduate with a degree in business economics and law. Despite her excellent grades and outstanding communication skills, she was rudely awakened when she found that looking for a job was very difficult in a recessionary economy. Anxious to find a job in the accounting or financial area, she networked by talking with her parents' personal tax accountant. He was able to give her names of members in the major professional society in her field of interest, as well as refer her to fellow accountants who were looking for entry-level employees.

Use the form to record the names of your professional advisers.

2. Expand Your Network

After you identify your existing network, you can begin to expand it. Discuss your goals with your primary contacts, and ask them if they know anyone who can advise

Professional Advisers

Name	Address	Phone	E-mail	Comments

you. The people to whom your primary contacts refer you are called secondary contacts, and they are more likely to be the ones who give the most important clues for your search. Of course, a network of contacts can be built *ad infinitum*. Your brother's mechanic may give you a tip for your job search. The permutations are endless.

Once your goal has been established, get in touch with personal contacts, primary, secondary and so on. You should mention your goal in the beginning of the conversation so that you don't forget to broach the topic. Some of your personal contacts will appreciate your straightforward approach. On the other hand, be sure to contact your friends and acquaintances even when you do not have a favor to ask; otherwise, they may form the impression that you call only when a favor is needed.

Susan and Mohammed dreamed of owning their own business for several years. They were able to locate a business by expanding their network. Initially, they tried a bookbinding business, which Susan's father had started. When that business did not sustain itself, they looked at many other opportunities, including fast-food restaurants, printing shops, and dry-cleaning outlets. Eventually they talked to some long-time friends about their desire to run a flower shop. As it happened, their friends had a brother who was looking for someone to buy his florist business. Susan and Mohammed started a partnership with their friends and bought the flower shop from their friend's brother.

Directories

You can build your contact list by choosing names from association directories, company telephone books, alumni listings, and even the public telephone book. Use the

Sources for Networking   69

reference section of the library to find the job marketplace directories. If you do not find a directory suited to your career search, try the *Encyclopedia of Associations* published by Gale Research. It lists more than 30,000 national and international organizations including professional associations for almost every job category, from farmers to international bankers. A directory that lists names in your specific field will be more useful than a public telephone book.

Locate the directory of the major professional association in your target area and write down the names of the officers of the association. The officers of a professional organization will encourage you to join and participate in their organization; they understand that networking is an important reason for people to get involved. Once you make contact with them, find out when the organization meets and attend a meeting.

3. Join Organizations and Volunteer

You can easily multiply your contacts by joining one or several organizations. Participate in the organization's activities and, better yet, volunteer to be a leader or officer for your professional society, club, church, or charity. All volunteer organizations rely on the willingness of their members to be leaders, to run activities, plan programs, and lead board meetings. By volunteering, you serve several purposes: you promote the goals and activities of the organization, you gain leadership skills and confidence, and you become more visible, increasing the likelihood of making valuable personal contacts.

If you enjoy meeting people, you may become the club's hospitality chair; if you can balance a checkbook, you can be the group's treasurer; if you take good notes, be the secretary. The reverse can work as well. If you are shy and want to make yourself meet new people, volunteering to be the membership chairperson may be the perfect opportunity to help gain confidence and help the club at the same time.

The act of volunteering is easy, but fulfilling your volunteer position can take many hours of your limited free time. Of course, your personal sacrifice should be outweighed by the positive benefits you receive. Volunteer positions give considerable psychological rewards and many opportunities for personal growth, as well as establishing new contacts.

Professional Societies

Professional societies are fertile ground for making contacts because their viability as a group depends on their ability to help members network successfully. Besides their educational function, most professional societies encourage networking, have special cocktail hours devoted to it, and act as a clearinghouse for job openings in the field.

For instance, the local chapter of my professional organization, the Society for Technical Communication (STC) makes an outstanding effort to help its members through networking. At its monthly dinner meetings, the STC offers a list of the job openings in the area on paper and on its web site. Companies and job agencies regularly call in their vacant positions so that this monthly listing is an accurate and timely reflection of the job market. Before the speaker of the evening is introduced, the president of the chapter begins the formal networking by asking new dinner guests to introduce themselves and to state whether they are looking for a job or offering a job. The networking portion of the meeting may take up to a half hour as people introduce themselves and announce job openings or their availability for a job opening. For senior members and new members alike, the networking portion of the meeting is always enlightening.

When my friend Mary was suddenly laid off from her company, one of her job-hunting strategies was to attend the next meeting of her professional organization and to use its job listing to help map potential employers. Within five weeks, she had multiple job offers. Her affiliation with the professional society made job-hunting much easier because she had a current listing of job openings in her field.

Many professional associations maintain databases or binders of their members' résumés that other members or local businesses can consult to fill job openings. The Business Professional Advertising Association's monthly newsletter features a networking column that lists positions available, specifying the title and qualifications of the job, and positions sought, describing the candidate's experience.

Through opportunities for continuing education and networking, you will benefit from joining your professional society. Depending on your profession, you can join several different professional organizations, each with its own special focus or niche. For example, if you are a property manager, you can join both the Property Management Association of America or the International Facility Management Association.

Specialized professional organizations exist for women, ethnic or religious affiliations, education, and more. The author of *Networking,* Mary Scott Welch, lists thirteen pages of networking organizations, including the following examples:

- Career Advancement Network, Columbus, Ohio

Professional Organization Contacts

Name	Address	Phone	E-mail	Comments

- Networks Unlimited, New York, New York
- River Oaks Breakfast Club, Houston, Texas
- The Career Network, Everett, Washington
- The Open Network, Denver, Colorado
- Math/Science Network, Oakland, California

Use the sheet to track the contacts you make through professional organizations.

4. Collect Business Cards

Attend as many social, educational, and business events as you can and collect business cards. When you prepare to go to conventions, meetings, and parties, bring a stack of your own cards and be prepared to meet others and collect their cards. If your company does not provide business cards, have your own made by a local printing shop. Many printers have special offers through which they will make 1,000 cards for about $30. If you want a card with a custom design or colored ink, you can expect to pay from $50 to $100 for 1,000 cards.

When you go to social or professional events, offer your business card to the people you meet and then ask for their business cards. If the person does not have a business card, take out one of your own and ask the person to write his business address on yours. Always make the information needed to contact you available to others, and you will increase your chances of making a worthwhile connection.

After the function is over, jot down where you met the person on the back of the business card and whether he or she has any special interests or background. Put these cards in your business card file or Rolodex. If you do not have a business card file, invest in one so that you have a convenient system to look up names, phone numbers, and addresses.

5. Learn to Introduce Yourself to Strangers

If you are a little shy, as most of us are, you could be saying to yourself "It's fine for other people to make contacts at social events, cocktail parties, and business seminars, but it is not for me."

Few people will go to a function where they don't know anyone. There seems to be nothing worse than trying to mingle in a room full of strangers and to be ignored or snubbed. To avoid this scenario, ask a friend or acquaintance to attend a social function with you. With this buddy system, you can more freely go out and meet new people. When, or if, you tire of initiating conversation, you can return to your friend for company. You can also make an agreement with your friend that she or he is to introduce you to someone and you are to reciprocate.

Unfortunately, you cannot always find a friend or acquaintance available for a social or business function, so it's important to learn to socialize by yourself. You can make socializing less awkward if you go to the event with a strategy in mind. Attend the event determined to meet some new and interesting people. Consider it a challenge and an adventure. Don't dwell on negatives.

One trick is to pretend that you are the host of the function and it is your responsibility to ensure that the guests are having a good time. Offer your hand to someone you don't know, and say something like this, "Let me welcome you. I'm so and so. What's your name?" The person replies. "So, Brian, are you enjoying yourself?"

Tell the person briefly about yourself, such as, what you do and what firm you work for. This gives the person an immediate context and will help put the person at ease. If you were the manager of a catering service, you might say, "I'm Vanessa Parnelli, owner of Parnelli Catering Service." You have not only introduced yourself, but you have also identified your market or niche. Now that the person knows you have a catering service, the person may think of you the next time she or someone she knows needs a catering service.

The author of *Conversationally Speaking,* Alan Garner, says you can start a conversation in three ways: talking about the situation ("It's awfully crowded here, isn't it? Where did you get the fruit salad?"); talking about yourself ("I'm a vendor from Boston."); or talking about the other person ("Where are you from? How are you enjoying tonight's program?") You can break the ice by asking questions, giving your opinion, or stating an observation.

Try starting a conversation with new people; it is not as hard as it sounds. Pay special attention to the body language of strangers to make sure you select a person open to conversation. Playing the role of the host is fun and extremely effective in overcoming your shyness and making new contacts. I met my husband this way. He was visiting a professional association for the first time. It was our election meeting and I was running for the board of directors. In this situation, I actually was an unofficial host of the organization and wanted to ensure that, as a newcomer, he would feel welcome.

If this technique does not work well for you the first few times, do not be discouraged. Overcoming shyness takes practice and a positive social environment. Look carefully for supportive and friendly groups, such as Toastmasters clubs, churches, softball leagues, or the service organizations and try this technique consistently until you feel comfortable. Also, practice the technique at small group meetings, such as a community college class or a church group, before tackling a social event with hundreds of strange faces.

Serious networkers use the "host the party" technique frequently and find that it makes mingling easier because they have a definite agenda when attending a social or business function. Politicians continually work a room out of necessity. When a person is running for mayor, he or she cannot afford to be shy. When the candidate goes into a room full of strangers, he or she sees a room full of potential voters, financial backers, and campaign volunteers. Politicians must make critical contacts for votes and for help in winning an election. When they enter a reception, party, company picnic, or Fourth of July parade, they network. Most of us do not need to meet every person at a social function; make your goal manageable, such as meeting three or four new people at every social event.

The Contact Sheet

As you begin building your network, review your goals and match your networking contacts to your objectives. Use the following worksheet to record your goal and the possible contacts who can help you. Copy the following page and use it to complete your worksheets on contacts.

Contact Sheet

Date: _____

Name: _____
Company: _____
Phone (O): _____
E-mail (O) _____
Address (O): _____
_____
_____

Phone (H): _____
E-mail (H): _____
Address (H): _____
_____
_____

Referral Source: _____
Outstanding Feature: _____
Notes: _____
_____
_____
_____
_____

Referrals Received: _____
_____
_____
_____
_____

A Friend and Contact Forever

Once you make a contact, keep it. You never know when you will need a contact made many years before. Ideally, you will keep contacts up to date on your progress; at the very least, do not throw away your lists. This is one area in which you should become a pack rat. Keep the directories from the schools you attended, and phone lists from companies where you once worked, and from clubs to which you once belonged.

Summary

Identify your existing network by examining your family, friends, teachers, classmates, co-workers, vendors, social acquaintances, neighbors, professional society members, and so on. Use these primary contacts to generate more contacts by asking them to refer you to their contacts. Often a secondary or tertiary contact, the proverbial friend of a friend, will refer you to the right opportunity that will fulfill your goal. Strangers and weak contacts, rather than close contacts, generally yield the best results.

You can increase your networking sources by joining organizations and volunteering for leadership positions. By increasing your visibility in this manner, you enhance your personal image and increase your opportunities for making contacts. Finally, at social and business events, learn to introduce yourself to strangers and collect as many business cards as possible for future reference. You can never have too many business cards and contacts.

If you follow these steps, your network will be in place and ready as you embark on your next business or personal quest.

4

Informational Interviewing

> *Although sharing information and contacts is their main purpose, networks can go beyond the mere transfer of data to the creation and exchange of knowledge. As each person in a network takes in new information, he or she synthesizes it and comes up with other, new ideas.*
>
> John Naisbitt, Megatrends

In the last chapter you learned how to build and expand your network. After you have established a clear goal, you can use your networking sources to do information gathering or, in networking jargon, informational interviewing.

Informational interviewing is ideal for people who are making a career transition, starting their careers, or thinking about moving to a new geographical area. Maybe you have worked in the financial area of a company for five years, but you want to get into market research. Or, for fifteen years you were a homemaker and you now want to learn about becoming a travel agent. Or you have lived your entire life in the city and are considering moving to a smaller, more rural location. Informational interviewing can help you to identify suitable careers or work environments and to generate actual job leads.

In informational interviewing, you interview a person in your desired field for information. Like an investigative reporter for a major city newspaper or a regional magazine, you want to get the inside scoop on one particular industry and, specifically, one profession. But unlike an investigative reporter, you do not publish your findings for the public. Rather, you use the material from your informational interview to build knowledge of the field and to cultivate personal contacts that can land you a job.

Assume you are interested in a specific career, such as hotel management. You have done library research, read trade journals and textbooks about the field, and taken college classes or even majored in the subject. Still, you don't have an insider's understanding of the field, and you have few job leads. You can learn about a career from first hand accounts and acquire concrete job leads at the same time by informational interviewing. You can also use informational interviewing to research a move to another town. When Bonnie wanted to research a move out of state, she used a short letter and a questionnaire to query her subjects about living in the other state, because the cost of doing a live interview would have been prohibitive.

My first attempt at informational interviewing came when I was a senior in college. As graduation crept closer, I began making frequent trips to the career counseling center to try to find my niche in a world of endless and complicated possibilities. The counselors handed me a copy of *Informational Interviewing,* a booklet by Bob Ginn, the director of Harvard's career placement office. The booklet described a systematic way of interviewing people directly to learn about a particular career or company. This information-gathering exercise is networking at the bare bones and can be an exciting learning experience. Because I was a liberal arts major and did not have a clear-cut objective, I went out and interviewed lawyers, college administrators, publishers, editors, business consultants, managers, and all sorts of professionals to find out what their working lives were like. It helped me to figure out a partial answer to that inevitable question, "What would you like to do when you grow up?"

Informational interviewing gives you a chance to learn more about your ideal careers, and more importantly can give you solid leads toward a professional job and career. It will help you begin to understand that making contacts is an important part of an overall career strategy.

On an informational interview, you visit a company site and see what the job environment is like; you talk with your personal contact — an insider, a person who manages or performs the job in which you're interested. Through informational interviewing you get a more realistic view of your envisioned career. Michele, a second-level manager at a medium-sized corporation, manages about thirty-five employees and has four managers reporting to her. Michele has been helping newcomers to the publishing field for many years and acts as a mentor for many of her employees. On informational interviewing, she notes, "Through being at the actual site, you'll learn more about the workplace. Most people can't imagine what it's like by reading textbooks. You need to get an inside look at how companies really work. Sometimes you'll find that you really wouldn't be happy working in a particular environment."

A couple of variations on informational interviewing — peer interviewing and "interviewing friendlies" — are described by Steve Cohen and Paulo de Oliveira in *Getting to the Right Job*. In peer interviewing, you speak to entry-level or junior people in the field in which you are interested. In interviewing friendlies, you learn to identify people who are sympathetic to your cause (your older cousin, your roommate's brother-in-law, and so forth) and interview them for possible job-related information.

The revelations you gain from informational interviewing will either make you further committed to your goal or convince you to look at a different area. In either case, informational interviewing will expand the scope of your possibilities and often help make actual job leads.

Some of those job leads will never be advertised or even posted internally, while others could be advertised in the future. By conducting the informational interview, you get a closer look at those positions by talking to people who work for the firm. If you have a good rapport or the right "chemistry" that mixes well with the person who you are interviewing, you can ask your personal contact to suggest other contacts who would give you an additional perspective of the industry. If your personal contacts give you the names of their contacts, you have succeeded in expanding your list of industry-knowledgeable people and have gained a personal reference with relatively little effort.

Informational Interviewing versus Job Interviewing

Informational interviewing has several steps in common with job interviewing, such as writing letters, preparing your résumé, and holding the interview. In both cases, you will want to dress appropriately and to present a positive personal image. Unlike a job interview, however, you do not want to get a job out of the informational interview (although this can be an unexpected bonus). In the informational interview, you are actively listening to industry experts — the manager of market research, the graphic designer, or the TV producer — and you're learning about their field, which may be the field that you want to pursue. Listen to your industry contact as an apprentice would listen to an experienced craftsperson. Because you are not asking for a job, there is little at risk. As one friend puts it, "You are not looking for a job, and the industry contact has not committed to hiring you. It's a win-win situation."

By contrast, the job interview is a riskier situation for both you and the company. In a job interview, your goal is to apply for a specific job opening. The company representative will be asking you questions and listening intently to what you say and how you say it. You must sell yourself and the company representative must sell the job to you. If the hiring manager interviews you properly, you should be talking eighty percent of the time.

In the informational interview, you are interviewing the industry expert. You will be asking the questions, and the industry expert will be responding. As you gather your information, your contact should be talking about eighty percent of the time, and you, like Barbara Walters or any other good interviewer, should be talking only twenty percent of the time.

In summary, here are the differences between the informational interview and the job interview:

Informational Interview
- Your goal is to learn about the industry and profession.

- You do not need to sell yourself as the right candidate for a particular job.
- You are asking questions and talking only twenty percent of the time.
- The industry expert is sharing his or her expertise and does not need to sell the company to you.

Job Interview
- Your goal is to apply for a specific job.
- You are answering the questions and talking eighty percent of the time.
- You are selling yourself.
- The company representative also must sell the company to you.

Informational interviewing and job interviewing do have similarities, as mentioned earlier. In both cases, you want to research the company and the contact person, you should dress appropriately, and bring a résumé and samples of your work. One cautionary note, however, is that some people feel you should not offer your résumé unless requested. They feel that bringing out your résumé makes you look like you are fishing for a job. On the other hand, I favor having a résumé prepared and available. Why? If I grant an informational interview, I want to assess your preparation, your education and your work experience for my field. A résumé will give me that information. Informational interviewing has these major steps:
1. Conducting the letter-writing campaign.
2. Preparing your résumé and job-related samples.
3. Making follow-up phone calls.

4. Researching the person and company to be interviewed.
5. Interviewing the industry expert.
6. Following up the informational interview.

1. Conducting the Letter-Writing Campaign

The first phase of informational interviewing is setting up your interviews through a letter-writing campaign, followed by a telephone call.

Conducting a letter-writing campaign is a nitty gritty part of informational interviewing, tedious but essential. First you'll need to compose a letter to introduce or re-introduce yourself to the industry contact. Make sure you spell the person's name correctly and correctly identify the person's gender. After all, some names are not gender-specific, such as Sam, Leslie, or Stacy. If you do not know how to spell the person's name or know the person's gender, call the person's company and ask the secretary for the correct spelling of the person's name, his or her gender, and the person's exact title. These instructions may sound obvious, but many people make the mistake of getting a person's name or gender wrong, and consequently, lose any possibility of receiving help from the offended party.

Here's a sample from a letter-writing campaign to arrange informational interviews. In this sample, a recent college graduate contacted an alumnus who was the editor of the company newsletter for a large firm.

Alexandra Burke
44 Emerson Street
San Francisco, CA 94309

August 16, 199x

John Hansen
1120 Pacific Heights Ave.
San Francisco, CA 94118

Dear Mr. Hansen,

    The alumni association gave me your name as an alumnus who is willing to talk to young graduates about jobs in their field. I graduated from the University of California at Santa Barbara in Communications. I have strong writing skills and would like to use those skills in industry. As editor of the company newsletter, you could give me considerable advice and insight into the field of business writing.

    Would you be able to meet with me briefly, perhaps for fifteen minutes, and give me some insight in this area? I will call next week to see when this might be convenient for you.

    I appreciate your help and hope to return the favor in some way if I have the chance.
Sincerely,

Alexandra Burke

Résumé attached for your information

Informational Interviewing

When you compose your letter of introduction, try to put yourself in the place of the recipient. If possible, think about what benefit you might give to the person you interview. The industry expert might be asking the proverbial "what's in it for me" question as he or she reads your letter. If possible, answer that question for your personal contact.

Of course, if you are inexperienced, it might be difficult for you to think of anything you could do for a seasoned professional. In the last example, because Alexandra was still quite new in the field when she contacted the alumnus, her letter was rather vague in this regard. But the sentence "I appreciate your help and hope to return the favor in some way if I have the chance" shows a sincere intent to have the contact be mutually beneficial.

How many letters and interviews should you set up? That depends on the number of good contacts you come up with, the amount of time you have, and how ambitious you are. The less experience you have in the job market, the more people you will need to contact and the more letters you'll probably want to write. Remember that, to a large extent, networking is a "numbers" game. The more people you write, call, and meet, the more likely you will make a contact that can give you the information required to meet your objectives. Don't be discouraged if it takes more than 100 letters and fifty or more ensuing interviews to get what you want. Realistically, it takes that much effort or more to match the right person to the right opportunity in the right place at the right time.

On average, you will write thirty to forty letters and conduct fifteen to twenty interviews. Not every letter results in an informational interview. Some people will flatly refuse because they are busy or are not interested in helping you. They might also misunderstand and believe you are looking for a job, saying "I'm sorry I can't meet with you. It's not a good time because we are having a hiring freeze." In such cases, you can respond, "I understand the situation, but I am not looking for a job. I am gathering information on a career, so the hiring freeze does not dampen my interest in meeting with you." Occasionally, the industry contact might defer you to a later time, such as three months down the road, when they are less busy or have returned from a vacation. Go with the flow, but be persistent.

If a person refuses to give you an interview, be polite. You might be able to contact the person at a later time and get a richly informative interview. Or if you detect that the person has absolutely no interest in helping, let it pass. Actress, author, and consultant Jan D'Arcy states that in any group of people, some will automatically want to help, some will be neutral, and others will automatically discount you. She advises that you need to find the people who are either disposed to help or those who are neutral. Simply ignore those who have already made up their minds not to help. Another tactic you might try is to ask the person for a better candidate to interview, perhaps someone with a more flexible schedule. Common sense dictates that it will be more difficult to get an informational interview with the CEO of a large corporation than with a lower-level manager or individual contributor, especially if you are just entering the field.

In some cases you will write many letters, but cannot follow up every letter with an interview because of time constraints or because you find a job after the third informational interview. If you decide not to set up the informational interview, let the person know through a phone call or a letter the reasons why your plans changed.

Some ambitious (and perhaps lazy) job-seekers recommend that you call rather than write to set up an informational interview. I recommend that you write a letter explaining your request instead of using a telephone call, for several reasons. Although a phone call is faster than a letter, a phone call could interrupt your contact at an inopportune moment. If you make the call, clearly you are calling at your convenience, and it might put your personal contact on the defensive. He or she might not immediately realize who you are, and what you want. Informational interviewing, while not unusual, is not generally a daily occurrence.

A letter is less intrusive than a phone call, it allows the personal contact to respond to you at his or her convenience, or to wait for your follow-up phone call. A letter also allows you to include your résumé so that the industry expert can get a better idea of who you are, what you have accomplished so far, and what you want to achieve. Busy managers are more likely to grant a request for an informational interview if they feel your background warrants their time.

Most of us know what it feels like to be interrupted by pesky salespeople or, even worse, to be solicited by an impersonal automatic phone machine. You do not want your phone call to be categorized with such phone nuisances. A well-written, personal letter requesting an informational interview and a neatly presented résumé can introduce you much more graciously than an out-of-the-blue phone call.

If you feel writing a letter is too old-fashioned, you can also fax your résumé and a brief explanation. Alternatively, you might get more immediate attention through an expressed letter or by sending an electronic mail message if you are willing to pay for those services or have them readily available. Times are changing; a century ago, when a person went to visit a stranger, he would often carry a letter of introduction or at least a business card of a mutual friend. When he arrived at the door, he could present the letter of introduction to the butler, who would allow him to wait in a sitting room while he whisked the letter to the mistress of the house.

After the mistress of the house read the letter of introduction, she could warmly welcome him to her home or business. Your letter requesting an informational interview is a modern day translation of that scenario. Now, however, instead of asking your mutual acquaintance to write a letter, you simply write the letter yourself. Of course, if you do have a good friend who is willing to write a letter or make a phone call for you, take advantage of the offer. The intervention of a mutual acquaintance can expedite the process and win you instant acceptance.

Sometimes, cold-calling can be effective for people who have a strong ego and are willing to do it. Lars, a business analyst from Denmark, was working for a Danish firm in the United States. His company told him he must return to Denmark if he wished to remain with the firm. Lars wanted to stay in the United States so he began making cold calls to prospective businesses. As a citizen of another country, he knew he would have to be aggressive in pursuing a job because he had a legal obstacle that United States citizens do not. He would need to have his employer fulfill the rules and regulations required by the Immigration and Naturalization Service to hire a foreign national. These rules are complicated, and many companies are reluctant to hire foreign nationals for that reason.

Through his cold calling, he was eventually able to make the right contacts to land a job at a reputable firm and retained the legal right to stay in the United States. Lars used networking so successfully that he feels that "getting a job in the United States is a piece of cake."

2. Preparing Your Résumé and Job-Related Samples

You should attach a résumé with your contact letter. Because your résumé summarizes your education and work experience, it gives your industry contacts the information they need to be able to advise you.

Your résumé is "your life on paper" so make sure that you make it attractive and interesting. It should market your skills and abilities so that a company will jump at the chance to hire you. If you find it difficult to market yourself effectively, ask for help from co-workers, friends, or family. Put your most impressive or important credentials first. Use active and specific verbs (manage, direct, create, design, develop and so on) to describe your experience.

Your résumé should be brief, ideally one page. If you have extensive experience, consider a one-page summary and a two- or three-page résumé. Make sure your résumé is letter perfect. Because it's not easy to be your own proofreader, seek help from family members, friends, or a professional résumé service.

If you have not prepared a résumé before and need more information, consult a reference book on the subject for more instructions. Here is a sample résumé:

John J. Lawrence
1234 Shady Hill Lane
Dallas, TX 94309
703-134-9876

Objective

A product marketing position in a corporate environment.

Work Experience

Software developer and support, Burroughs Corporation, Los Angeles, 1967 to 1977.

Program manager, NCR Corporation, San Diego and Wichita, Kansas, 1977 to 1983.

Software product manager, Atari, Inc., San Jose, 1983 to 1987.

Product marketing manager, Texas Instruments, Dallas. 1987 to present.

Education

B.A. in English, cum laude, Brown University, 1967.

Graduate courses in computer science and business at University of California, Los Angeles. 1968 to 1972.

Honors and Interests

Dallas Lions Club, 1987 to present.

Richardson Business League, Board of Directors, 1988 to present.

References available on request

In addition to your résumé, you need to prepare job-related samples. Send a brief sample and bring more with you to the interview.

What exactly are work-related samples? For any specific field, consider what, if any, tangible output the typical profession makes and prepare your own samples. These samples could be case histories, research, legal briefs, technical reports, spreadsheets, videotapes. Ideally, the samples should be real, but they can also be the result of coursework in the field or just your best efforts. For example, many aspiring advertising copywriters and graphic artists mock up sample ads that they have written or designed and present them in a portfolio. If you are interviewing a television producer, you might prepare a videotape of your community or college productions. If you are interviewing the vice president of a software development firm, you might prepare some sample programs you have written.

As a technical writer, I have a portfolio that contains examples of memos, procedures, and manual excerpts that I have written or edited. A particularly effective sample for any field is a before and after piece, showing what material you were given to work with and how you developed it.

You can present your samples in a professional designer portfolio available from an artist supply store. If you are an artist, model, or a designer, this is a wise investment. Alternatively, you can simply bring writing samples, photographs, video or audio tapes in your briefcase and pull them out at the appropriate moment. Your personal contact might want to look at your samples at a later time, so if possible, bring a sample to leave behind.

Also bring letters of reference or recommendations from previous employers or professors, and a note from a mutual acquaintance if you have them. These letters generally state how the reference knows you and what qualities you can bring to a job. While glowing letters are appreciated, a positive letter from a well-respected teacher or manager can be more impressive.

3. Making Follow-up Phone Calls

You have mailed your letters and résumés and prepared job-related samples and letters of reference. In rare instances, one of your contacts will call and set up an appointment. More likely, you will follow up your letter with a telephone call. Because you are asking your contact for a favor, it's up to you to take the initiative and follow through.

Try to phone your personal contact one or two days after you expect your letter has arrived. You don't want to wait so long that the person could have read your letter and then forgotten about it.

What to say in your phone call to the personal contact is often the most difficult moment in informational interviewing. It takes courage to break the ice, especially if you have never met the person, but were simply referred by a mutual acquaintance. It may take a considerable effort to make this phone call. At times like these, just do it. Take a philosophical "stiff drink" and make the phone call.

In some cases, calling the personal contact is rather matter of fact. In the case of Alexandra (see the letter on page 75), she expected her personal contact to be cordial to her request because he volunteered to counsel other alumni. In this example, not only did John give Alexandra an interview and a tour of his company, he also later took her to lunch.

In other cases, you might never have met the contact, and will not know in advance how the person will react to

Informational Interviewing

your request. You will rightfully be reluctant to make that first phone call because you may get a rejection. On the other hand, you may be warmly received. If you were referred by a mutual friend, your chances of success are higher.

In any doubtful cases, practice with a script. However, do not be so well-rehearsed that you sound stilted and unnatural. Here's a sample conversation of a person following up a letter and asking for an informational interview:

> "Susan [name of the contact], my name is John Lawrence [your name]. I'm a friend of David Wentz [your mutual contact], president of the Shaker Heights Business Association. I hope you received the letter I sent you last week.... You did? Good. I'd like to meet you some time at your convenience to discuss opportunities in product marketing [your field]. When would be a good time for you?"

If the person has not received your letter, you must explain your request over the phone. If you notice some hesitation in the voice of your personal contact, you can reassure the person that the interview will be brief, fifteen minutes or so. Or you might suggest that you contact them in a few days when they are less busy.

Remember to take the initiative and call to set up an appointment. Many opportunities will be wasted if you do not establish contact. Networking is not a passive waiting game; only an active, go-for-it attitude will make networking work.

When you phone for an interview, you might find that your subject prefers to talk to you over the phone rather than meet. While you gain significantly more information through a personal interview, a telephone interview can be a quick and efficient way to gather information. In this case, prepare a list of questions in advance so you can conduct the telephone interview smoothly. Suggested questions are listed later in the chapter.

4. Researching the Person and Company to be Interviewed

If you prepare well for the interview, through researching the person and company to be interviewed, your informational interview will undoubtedly be more successful. By doing your homework, you won't fumble by asking questions that are naive or embarrassing. Before you even consider informational interviewing in a field, you should have already researched the field. This means reviewing trade journals in the area, textbooks, and other related materials. If possible, you will have taken a few college or adult education courses related to the field as well.

To research the person and company you are contacting, start with the library or the Internet. If the company is a public organization (that is, it sells stock to the public, like General Electric, Citibank, or Sears), you can get information that is mandated by the Securities and Exchange Commission. With a little digging at the reference desk and in the reference bookshelves, you can find financial information, credit ratings, and newspaper and magazine articles about the company, its product line, and its chief personnel. And if you really have moxie, you can pretend to be a prospective stockholder and call a stockbroker for an assessment of the company's past and its future earnings and growth.

If the company is private, but still large, or previously public, you will probably be able to find similar but less

Informational Interviewing

detailed information. If the company is a small, private firm, you will probably have to rely on the company itself to provide information. Whether the company is private or public, it sells some goods or services to the retail or business trade. Thus, the company will probably have marketing materials, such as advertisements, data sheets, catalogs, or order forms. You can pretend you are a potential customer and call the company for such information. If the company is public, you can also call its public relations, marketing, or investor relations department and get a copy of its latest annual report.

Some of you might balk at my suggestion to pretend to be a prospective stockholder or customer. If pretending makes you feel uncomfortable (as harmless as the pretense is), you can simply say you are doing research on the company for an upcoming interview. In this case, contact the personnel or human relations department for information.

5. Interviewing the Industry Expert

You have found your industry expert, sent your letter and résumé, prepared your job-related samples, researched the person and the company, and set up the appointment. Finally the big day of your informational interview arrives. Make sure you do the following:

- Dress for the job you want or a little better.
  Dress appropriately for the interview. If people in the field wear pin-striped suits, then dress that way for the interview. On the other hand, if people in the field dress in flannel shirts and blue jeans, dress that way. Your previous research should help you determine what the company culture calls

for, a suit or less formal attire. Even if you are interviewing at an informal company, being dressed a little more formally than your personal contact generally does not hurt your image.
- Be on time.
- Be polite; don't be too stiff or too casual.
- Be friendly and natural.
- Avoid personal topics.
  Don't talk about personal topics, such as marital status, religious or political affiliations, sports, and so on unless you are certain your subject is interested in the topic and will not use the information against you. For instance, if you notice a tennis trophy in the office of your personal contact and you share an interest in tennis, it will probably help you to mention this. Otherwise, don't do it.
- Have a strong handshake and practice it.
- Be as professional as possible from the moment you walk in the door of the company; even the receptionist can work for or against your success.

Give yourself a pep talk. What you lack in experience might be compensated for with enthusiasm. Have a clear objective in mind. In the informational interview, you are looking for cooperation, advice, support, and referrals; you are not looking for a job.

Before you go, prepare a list of questions. These should be open-ended to allow your industry expert to speak at some length. For example, you could ask these questions:

- How did you get started in this field?
- What do you like most about this field?
- How do you spend your time on a daily or weekly basis? What activities do you do, and what percentage of time is spent on each activity?
- What would you like to change about this field?
- What types of challenges do you encounter?
- What advice would you give to a newcomer?
- How can I better prepare to enter this field?
- What books or publications should a newcomer read?
- What other people in this field do you suggest I talk with for another valuable perspective?
- What personal attributes do you think are essential for success?
- Which professional journals and organizations should I know about?
- Could you give me a brief tour of a typical area I would work in?
- What skills are required to be successful as a [your desired profession]?
- Do you know of any companies that hire and train recent graduates?
- Do you know of any current openings appropriate for a person with my background?
- What would my earning potential be in the field?
- How well do you think my background and education would fit into this field?

- What is the reason most people choose this field? What reasons do people have for leaving?
- What opportunities do you see in the future of this field?
- If you had it to do over, would you enter this industry?

During the interview, you also might ask if your industry expert has any specific suggestions on how you could improve your résumé. At this time, you can bring up the fact that you brought job-related samples. If time permits, ask your personal contact if he or she would be interested in seeing them now. Alternatively, you could leave a copy of the sample for the person to look at later.

If you have made an excellent impression and the industry expert has a job opening, the person might interview you for a job right then and there. The manager might even be able to create a job even if there is no specific opening. I have known people who have obtained jobs or have had jobs created for them through informational interviewing. If you are interested in interviewing for a job, you can let the informational interview evolve into a job interview or offer to set up another meeting to interview for the particular job, especially if you need more preparation or simply want to keep the informational interview separate from a job interview. If you are not interested in interviewing for a job, restate your objective of gathering information only.

In preparing for an informational interview, anticipate the questions that your personal contact might ask. If the contact has the ability to hire, you might find that the informational interview becomes a job interview. Think ahead as to how you would answer typical job interview questions

should they arise. These questions include, but are not limited to:
- Tell me about yourself. (Remember to make your answer job-related.)
- What is your greatest strength?
- What is your weakest area?
- What do you plan on doing in five, ten, or twenty years?
- Why should I hire you?
- Do you work well under pressure?

For more information about preparing for a job interview, consult your local library or bookstore for a book specifically on job interviewing.

Like the job interview, the informational interview could last anywhere from five minutes to several hours. You'll remember that I suggested a short informational interview of fifteen minutes. The fifteen-minute interview is short enough that a person will have a hard time saying no, but long enough to get some valuable information and perhaps talk your way into a longer interview.

Most successful informational interviews, the ones that will lead to a job, last for forty-five minutes to an hour. If the industry contact believes your background suitable, and likes you, you might find yourself in a two-hour interview and on your way to a new job. Let your personal contact take the lead. If the person is comfortable and continues talking past the fifteen-minute length, enjoy the conversation and keep going. If, however, you get the cue to wrap up (your personal contact looks at the clock or begins to lose eye contact with you), begin to finish your conversation and thank the person for the interview.

Potential Problems During the Informational Interview

Some of your subjects will know exactly how to act during an informational interview; others will be uncomfortable and might need some direction. Here are some tips should you encounter these problems:
- Silence — Refer to your list of questions and be sure to ask open-ended questions (those that require more than a yes or no answer).
- Rude response — If you think the person is busy, thank the person and leave early or arrange another time. If you think the person does not understand the purpose of the interview, state that you want advice and information only, not a job.
- Lengthy answers — If you are benefiting from the information, let the subject talk. Otherwise, keep on track by emphasizing that you do not want to take too much of the person's valuable time, then ask another question.

6. Following up the Informational Interview

Following up the interview is as critical as the interview preparation and the interview itself. More people stumble here than at any other phase of making personal contacts. They fail to follow up consistently and regularly, so their personal contacts quickly forget about them.

After the interview, follow up with a note of thanks. So many people ignore this small courtesy that when you do remember, your hand-written or typed personal note will make you memorable. A follow-up phone call is also welcome, but should not be a substitute for a letter. And remember to thank not only the industry contact, but every person who helped in the process, including the secretary who let your call go through, the person who referred you, etc. Without them, their time, knowledge, and connections, you would never have succeeded.

If you obtain a job through your personal contact, be sure to call or write to let the person know about your progress. Thank him or her again and offer to take the person to lunch or dinner. If an offer of lunch or dinner seems inappropriate, you might send a gift or flowers.

I know a woman who is reluctant to grant informational interviews because of one experience with a recent college graduate who had relocated from another part of the country. She gave the young graduate a lengthy one-hour informational interview, giving him tips on how to present himself and his qualifications, and the name and phone number of another manager in her company who had an appropriate job opening. The young graduate wrote her a thank-you note for the informational interview, but he never told her that he had obtained the job to which she had referred him. When the young man interviewed with the hiring manager, he did not disclose who had referred him or explain how he happened to know so much about the company and the position. A few months later, the woman was flabbergasted when the college graduate was "introduced" to her as the company's new employee. The woman who had given the informational interview felt burned.

If you meet with any of the people suggested by your original personal contact, let the original contact know about your progress. Think of your contact not merely as a source of information, but as a personal friend who has taken valuable time to help you. The word to note here is "friend." By failing to remember those who help, you distinguish yourself as an ungrateful opportunist.

Emulate the successful car salesperson who sends his customers birthday cards, holiday cards, or appropriate notes to let them know he is their appreciative fan. If you read an article in a magazine that you think would be interesting to your contact, clip it and send it. If you do land a job in the field (with or without the person's help), let the person know of your success.

If you persistently maintain a contact, the contact becomes a friend and, if you are lucky, a mentor. Of course, there is a difference between pleasantly reminding a person of your needs and becoming a pest. Do not write or call only when you have a favor to ask. Keep in touch especially when you don't have any favors to ask. By nurturing the relationship, you ensure a long and fruitful friendship.

Also, follow up with people who do not result in personal interviews. Let them know the result of your information gathering because they might be curious about your progress. If you have not achieved what you set out to accomplish, your letter is another reminder that you still seek their assistance. Their circumstances may have changed and they may now know of an opening that is right for you.

Here are two sample letters: one is a follow-up letter after an informational interview and the other is a follow-up letter to a person contacted but not interviewed.

Danielle Barber
18 Vine Street
Cincinnati, Ohio 50166

March 19, 199x

David Abbott
Procter and Gamble
222 Oak Street
Cincinnati, Ohio 50167

Dear Mr. Abbott:

    Thanks so much for the informational interview and the tour of Procter and Gamble. I enjoyed learning about the public relations department of the company and am encouraged by your example.

    I appreciate your taking the time to meet with me and explaining the path that your career has taken. I wanted to let you know that I have settled down and found a job as a junior account executive with the Gray Advertising firm in Chicago. I hope to put my business skills and creative skills to work there.

    Please look me up if you are in the Chicago area. I've enclosed my business card.
Sincerely,

Danielle Barber

Bert Shigekawa
1123 Columbus Avenue, Apt. 105
New York, NY 12034

August 5, 199x

Ms. Molly Dickinson
Smith and Hernandez Manufacturers
345 Avenue of the Americas
New York, NY 12555

Dear Ms. Dickinson:

    Last month I sent you a letter about a possible information gathering interview. We were able to speak briefly on the phone, but were unable to schedule a meeting.

    I've been busy with interviews, both for jobs and information. And I'm happy to report that I am now working as a management consultant with McKinsey and Company. I apologize for not getting back to you sooner.

    I hope we'll have the opportunity to meet some time in the future.

Warmest regards,

Bert Shigekawa

Staying Organized

If you are conducting informational interviewing on a large scale, stay organized and use your time wisely. One networker I know suggests dividing your time. Meet people on even days of the month, and write letters and make follow up telephone calls on the odd days. On these days, you can use uninterrupted time to write thank-you notes and do whatever else is needed.

Keep details in order by using a notebook or a computer program to store information about contacts. Record notes of every major contact and the results from your interviews in a personal contact log. Your log should contain information about the contact's name, title, address, and telephone number as well as unique qualities, personal information, family background, education, and professional data, including interests, professional memberships, secretary's name, and so on. The next pages show a sample personal contact log.

Joan Kern
Kern Consultants
4451 Avenue of the Americas
New York, NY 02113
213-339-1112

Unique Characteristics
Joan has a very warm personality, puts people at ease immediately. She has a go-for-it attitude and is well-traveled.

Professional Information
- Board member of Women's Business Network of New York
- Teaches at New York University, does training in writing and presentation skills for local companies
- Friend of Bill Marquez
- Joan's secretary is Amanda. Amanda is friendly and loves to talk about her dogs

Personal Data
- Moved to US from Philippines at age 2, grew up on Long Island
- Husband: Martin Fenner, also consultant
- Daughter: Martina, 11 years old

Educational Background
Education: University of Michigan, master's degree in Speech Communications

Contact
Referred by Bill Marquez, Aunt Millie's friend

Aug. 6	Got address and no. from Bill Marquez
Aug. 16	Sent a letter, requesting informational. interview, to Joan
Aug. 23	Followed up with phone call. Left message.
Aug. 28	Joan calls back.
Aug. 31	Appoint at Joan's office. 10:00 am. Recommended I contact Tom Brown at Gray Advertising. Phone no. 213-123-1234.
Sept. 5	Sent thank-you note.

Other
- Told me about her husband's classmate, Tom Brown, who has an entry-level management job at his company, Crown Corporation.
- Invited me to attend her class at New York University at 7 am on Tuesday and Thursday mornings.
- Also a member of the Professional Women's Network of Long Island and the American Association of Training Professionals.
- Articles published in New York magazine.

On the Other Side of Informational Interviewing

As a networker, you will also be giving informational interviews. If you are a newcomer yourself, few people may ask for help at first. However, as you become more experienced, responsible, and visible, you can expect to hear from others who would like to interview you.

A networking aficionada, Michele has tips for being on the other side of informational interviewing. She writes, "When you receive a request to give an informational interview, analyze the request carefully. If you feel the person would get more direct information from another industry contact, redirect the person to the other industry contact. This will save time for both of you."

She advises that you schedule the informational interview ten days from when you receive the original request. On your appointment book, write the name of the person, a home and message phone, and the topic to be discussed. Schedule an hour appointment and arrange for no interruptions.

If the person has not already sent a résumé, ask the person for a current one before the interview. If the résumé arrives before the informational interview, spend some time preparing by writing down reference books, societies, contacts, buzzwords, and any other information that could help. If you do not receive the résumé, call the person and postpone the interview until it arrives.

State a goal at the beginning of the informational interview. For example, you can ask the interviewer to begin with three to five prepared questions about the field.

Review the questions and the person's résumé and relate your answers to the information at hand and to the job market as you know it. End promptly and summarize what was covered. Give the person a brief tour of the company as you walk the person out.

Put the person's résumé in a file called "Networking résumés" and write the date and a few remarks about the person. Expect a thank-you letter or phone call from the person. If you receive a thank-you note, decide if you think the person would fit well with any of the jobs available and route that person's résumé. If you don't receive a thank-you note, reconsider whether the person is worth helping any further.

Congratulate yourself. You have now graduated from asking for informational interviews to giving them yourself and have experienced informational interviewing from both sides. If you help others find jobs and establish their careers, your reputation will grow as a person who has contacts and can get things done.

Summary

You can use informational interviewing as a practical and effective tool for exploring a new career area, relocating to a new community, changing companies, or expanding your list of meaningful contacts. Short of getting a job in the area of your choice, informational interviewing gives you a clearer picture of what your desired profession or desired work environment is like. Unlike job interviewing, you and the industry contact you interview are under no great pressure. Yet, a number of informational interviews are likely to yield some job leads that may give you the inside track to job openings, some of which are never posted or advertised.

Does informational interviewing work? Ned, a former co-worker, found his mentor through informational interviewing. As a recent graduate from college, Ned asked an alumnus for an informational interview. The alumnus took special interest in Ned's endeavors. He gave him an extensive list of contacts in fields such as banking, commodities trading, and stock brokerage. Ned got his first job at a financial institution through his mentor's efforts. However, after six months of working as an analyst, he felt dissatisfied. Fortunately, he was able to call a friend of his mentor in the commodities trading field and land a job in that industry. He is now a successful commodities trader.

As you gain experience and reputation in your own field, you will be on the other side of informational interviewing, giving informational interviews to newcomers. Encourage and maintain both your newcomer contacts and your industry expert contacts; they will become part of your expanding professional network and potentially part of your circle of personal friends.

5

Networking on the Internet

> *What the Net offers is the promise of a new social space, global and antisovereign, within which anybody, anywhere, can express to the rest of humanity whatever he or she believes without fear.*
> — *John Perry, cofounder*
> *Electronic Frontier Foundation*

Networking in person will always have greater impact than networking electronically, but when you network on the Internet, you can have a global reach, mass access, and split-second response time. Electronic networking has transformed the nature of social interactions. Just as telephones revolutionized interpersonal communications earlier, the Internet has revolutionized person-to-person networking and the job search.

What is the Internet? In the simplest terms, the Internet is an international network of computer networks. Your computer, at home or on the job, can be connected with other computers all over the world. With a few taps on the keyboard, you can send and receive messages and files with text, graphics, audio and video. The most popular applications on the Internet are electronic mail (e-mail), Usenet news, and the World Wide Web. Other applications include Internet Relay Chat (IRC), file transfer protocol (FTP), Gopher, Telnet, Archie, and Veronica. We will briefly cover the top three Internet programs: electronic mail, Usenet news, and the World Wide Web.

Even if you don't own a computer, you can try out the Internet. If you're relatively inexperienced, I recommend taking a class from your local community college, adult school or community center. If you're more adventurous, visit your local public library and find out where you can get free access; many libraries and city services offer public Internet access. Finally for about $10 an hour, visit a cyber-cafe. Internet cafes are listed in the telephone directories.

What Does the Internet Provide?

The Internet provides functions in these four broad categories:
- A global library
- A forum
- A message center
- An entertainment and news center

The Internet is a global library. You may not be able to find the text of every published book there, but you can get the complete works of William Shakespeare, the annotated Bible, the card catalog of the Library of Congress, maps of most places in the world (including your own neighborhood), recipes, up-to-date stock market reports, and the latest real estate listings. Should you get bored with any of the above, you can also find foreign language dictionaries, information on every major city in the United States and the world, catalogs and general information from schools, colleges, and universities, and marketing literature and job openings for almost all of the world's major corporations. The Internet is a forum — a place for people to gather online. There are real-time events on the Internet: job fairs, artist and writer networks, and town hall meetings. You can participate in 20,000 discussion groups, called Usenet news groups. The Internet has a Usenet news group on practically any topic you can imagine from computers to zoology, and Afghanistan to Vietnam. Job seekers and job changers will find Usenet news groups devoted to listing and discussing job opportunities in geographic regions, including New York, San Jose, Paris and Hong Kong.

Those of you who are not yet cruising the Internet may wonder if people really meet online. Yes, the advice columns like Ann Landers and Dear Abby are true. People do meet and become friends online. When I was researching a column on electronic mail, I corresponded with a couple who had met on a Usenet news group. He was a graduate student in Boston; she was an undergraduate at the University of Oregon. After several months of e-mail, they met in his hometown in Florida. They soon became engaged and were married in her hometown in the Pacific Northwest.

The Internet is a message center, a combination post office and telephone party line. As a post office, the Internet far surpasses traditional mail, or "snail mail" as Internet fans call it. The Internet is the information superhighway, carrying e-mail messages around the world in seconds. If you don't currently use e-mail, once you get started you will find that the price of your Internet service is worth every dime, just to use this single application. E-mail is a far more convenient and effective way to communicate than the telephone (you have a written record) or regular mail (you just type your message on the computer, and zap!).

When a neighbor's daughter moved from Palo Alto, California, to the Middle East to attend college, he and his wife worried about the cost of keeping in touch. Instead of running up expensive phone charges, the Tamlers got an online service to send e-mail to their daughter almost daily. Howard says, "Postal mail usually takes one to two weeks and the telephone is inconvenient because of the time zone difference." He adds, chuckling, "Now we can bicker endlessly over her summer travel plans for less than $10 a month."

Besides being a very fast post office, the Internet can also act as a telephone or chat line. You can "talk" to people on the Internet in real time. Internet Relay Chat is a program that enables you to type in your comments to others and get a response right away. In addition to IRC, many online services have public chat rooms, as well as private chat rooms where you can hold a personal and private conversation. Some of the public chat rooms become silly and outrageous, but there are chat rooms for specific ages and interests for more focused discussions. Many special interest groups have online chats dealing with a specific topic, such as career advancement or parenting. Some rooms host famous TV stars or authors.

In these chats, you can enter a question and get a response from the other person online as if you were conversing. Online chats have the disadvantage of slowness (most folks can talk a lot faster than they can type), but they are a wonderful opportunity to meet people worldwide and converse with them in real time for a fraction of the cost of long-distance video-conferencing or telephone.

The Internet is an entertainment and news center. With a fast modem, you can get Internet News Radio or Thailand Digital music right out of your computer speakers. There is video entertainment, including soap operas made especially for the Internet. You can even get newspapers and magazines on the Internet. You can look up old articles and print them out, which is a lot neater than keeping stacks of papers in your garage. My favorite part is you don't get ink all over your fingers!

If you've moved away from your hometown, you can look up your hometown daily and get the latest news on your old neighborhood. You can find hundreds of magazines online from *Time* to *Good Housekeeping*. However, many of the online magazines do not carry the exact same versions as their newsstand equivalents. Articles are sometimes condensed and advertisements are far less prominent. In addition to traditional magazines and papers, there are many newsletters, magazines, and papers that are created for the Internet with no equivalent non-Internet form. Because information is so much easier to assemble and disseminate electronically, thousands of small operators, the "mom and pop" shops of the online world, are hosting web sites to share their vacation photos or sell their homemade jams. Their information is as easily accessed as the most sophisticated web site of some gigantic multinational corporation.

The Internet is great for game enthusiasts: You can play dungeon and dragon-type games interactively with someone on the other side of town or the other side of the world. There are virtual-reality games, chess, checkers, puzzles, comics, word games, and joke-of-the-day sites.

What Makes the Internet Different

Although the Internet is like many other forms of media you know and understand, it has many qualities that make it unique. The Internet differs from other media, like TV, newspapers, books, and movies in that it is fast, open, and low-cost.

The Internet is fast. You can send an e-mail message to a business associate in Spain and get a response by e-mail in a few seconds. If you are researching a possible move to North Carolina, post a message on a Usenet news group and, within a few days, you'll hear from people with their tips, suggestions, and personal experiences. These people are complete strangers except for their commonality as an Internet user. Where else in the world can you ask a question and get as many responses quickly and free?

The Internet is open. People are networking on the Internet all the time, trading facts and information, opinions and stories. Because people are communicating through a machine (the computer) and feel somewhat protected, they are often more willing to give their opinion, positive or negative. For example, if someone came to your door and asked for your opinion on a controversial subject like abortion, you might be reluctant to say what you actually thought. Online, however, the interviewer is not standing on your front porch and may be on another continent (but you should be careful anyway). Communicating by computer feels semi-anonymous even though a computer hacker could break the shroud of privacy in minutes. Nevertheless, most people feel freer to converse online than on the telephone or in person.

Because communicating online takes little effort (once you're logged on), people often are more willing to share information. Consider the alternative. If you write to an expert requesting information, she has to be convinced your request is worth her efforts. To respond by letter, she has to type and print a letter, find a stamp, and then go to the post office. However, if you ask her for some information through e-mail or Usenet news, she need only type a few lines on a computer and press Return to send her message around the world to you.

Online communication has definite advantages, in that you're not judged by your race or your physical attributes. Old Internet users joke that, online, "no one can tell you're a dog." On the other hand, when you communicate on the Internet, you may be surprised by outbreaks of temper, called "flaming." Because people are more open to expressing their opinions, they may verbally attack you without fear that you'll punch them through the computer screen. They can also lie and you'll never be able to look directly at them to analyze their body language.

The Internet is low-cost. You can communicate globally inexpensively. Even if you don't own a computer, you can rent time at a cybercafe for around $10 (U.S.) an hour. You can use the Internet for free at many public libraries and some community centers. If you don't already have personal Internet access, the cost isn't overwhelming. For the minimal setup, you will need a computer; a modem; a telephone line; and an Internet server provider (around $20 a month for the service, plus any toll charges). If you don't mind having your telephone line busy when you're dialing into the Internet, you can use your regular line for the Internet as well as your telephone.

In addition to being fast, open, and low-cost, the Internet is also decentralized, dynamic, largely non-commercial, and growing rapidly. The Internet has no centralized control, but does have standards proposed by a voluntary membership organization, the Internet Engineering Task Force (IETF). Anyone can host a web site, and you can say almost anything on the Internet as long as it is not libelous. No individual, company, or country owns the Internet.

Many governments of the world, including the United States, Germany, and China, have grappled with how to control the Internet. Truly an experiment in freedom of speech, the Internet community must daily deal with complex legal issues, such as the propagation of copyrighted materials, and morally repugnant information, including obscene, pornographic, and hate literature. Parents or guardians need to supervise the use of the Internet by children just as they would supervise their use of the television and other media. The Internet is a public place and, as such, you need to be vigilant to scams and other criminal activity.

The Internet is dynamic and growing rapidly. No doubt you've heard the statistics bandied about. There are about ten million Internet users worldwide and the popular search directory Yahoo! predicts there will be 170 million users before the end of the century. It's difficult for an individual to sense the growth of the Internet; you can't really see it. However, you can gauge the growth by how often someone asks for your e-mail address and by how many web site addresses you see advertised in the media. If you really want statistics on the growth of web sites and users, you could look it up on the Internet.

The Internet has historically been non-commercial; it started in 1969 as an experiment called the Arpanet developed by the Advanced Research Projects Administration, part of the United States Department of

Defense. The original Arpanet connected only four institutions: the University of California at Santa Barbara, the University of Utah, SRI International, and the University of California at Los Angeles. In the 1970s and 1980s, the Arpanet grew to become the Internet, but it was still largely reserved for academic research and corporate communication. In the 1990s, commercial activity blossomed and has sometimes threatened to ruin the usability and commercial-free nature of the Internet. For the most part, information on the Internet is still free; you won't get charged to look at most web sites. Internet etiquette, known as "netiquette," suggests that companies not put advertisements in your face or send unsolicited sales pitches.

Getting Started with E-mail

To get started on the Internet, you need to understand a few concepts. If you want to use electronic mail, you'll need to have an electronic mail address. Like a telephone number, each e-mail address identifies an account. A standard e-mail address is formed like this:

username@domainname.domaintype

The domain name is the name of the computer network that supplies the e-mail service. The domain name for Oracle Corporation, a software maker, is oracle.com. The domain name for America Online, an online service, is aol.com. The domain name for Harvard University is harvard.edu. Each of these institutions has one or more domain names associated with it. Each domain also has an indicator as to its role:

.com is used for commercial companies
.gov is used for government agencies
.mil is for the military

.edu is for educational institutions
.net is for networks
.org is for non-profit organizations

E-mail addresses may also show a country code like .au (Australia), .il (Israel), .ca (Canada).

When you work at a company, you may be required to follow company convention for your e-mail address, or you may be able to choose your own. When you get a personal Internet service, you can create your own address as long as it is unique in the domain. Now that you understand e-mail addresses, you can start networking by e-mail, or you can become even more sophisticated by developing your own web page.

Creating a Web Page

Wouldn't it be great to have people find you on the Internet? Susan Roane, the self-proclaimed "mingling maven" and author of *How to Work a Room* says it's not only who you know, but "who knows you."

Help people to find you by distributing your business card and résumé and using an e-mail signature. Another creative way to market yourself is by having a web page on the Internet. When Roger Firestone lost his job with a large computer company, he used both traditional and non-traditional methods to advertise his availability. He called friends, previous managers, and colleagues. He e-mailed his contacts all over the United States. Finally, he learned HTML (HyperText markup language) to create his own web page. Firestone says the web has "been a convenient way of informing people about me and they can get my résumé even faster than by e-mail."

When you put your web site on the World Wide Web, people around the globe will be able to find you electronically. They may be potential clients and employers, old classmates, journalists, and perhaps even a long lost friend. You will need to learn HTML to create a web site. While HTML sounds a bit mysterious and technical, it's really not difficult, and it is a far cry from computer programming. If you already know how to use a computer and a word processor, you can create simple a web page in half a day. (For step by step instructions for creating your own web site, see Chapter Eight.)

Seeking Help

Pam Dixon, the author of *Be Your Own Headhunter Online,* warns that people should not pay high fees to get a simple home page on the Internet. She suggests that you call the local university's computer department or computer club. The Online Career Center offers home pages for job seekers and charges $40 for up to three pages of text, two graphics, and two links to other web sites for six months. If you want a fancy web site with programming and original graphics, however, you'll need to consult an experienced web designer.

When you create your web page, multimedia specialist Bill Hazzard advises, "Limit fancy graphics, colors, audio and video. You don't want your web site to take 45 minutes to load." Adds Comet, a technical support specialist, "Remember not everyone has a World Wide Web browser with graphics. Describe the graphic with the <ALT> tag so people with line mode browsers have an idea of what you're communicating."

In addition to putting your résumé on your web site, consider sharing other useful information related to your interests. Some people include articles they've written, excerpts from their Ph.D. dissertation, links to other web sites that they recommend, or just helpful information they've accumulated throughout the years.

Getting your web site on the World Wide Web and making your web page well-designed and useful is only half of the job. You'll also need to tell people about your web page. Steven Turner writes a note on every e-mail message he sends out. The note says, "Steven is actively looking for opportunities in the job market. What does he do? What does he know? Check out his home page on the WWW."

6

Using Electronic Mail, Listservs, and Usenet News

Electronic mail is text prepared on a computer and sent to another person who has an e-mail address or account. Electronic mail was used on private networks inside companies and schools for many years before the Internet became widely available. Now many of the private networks are connected to each other through the Internet. Thus, even if you're a scholar at Stanford University, you can send an e-mail message to a colleague at Cambridge University.

Although most e-mail accounts are still a resource provided by an employer or a school, more and more people are getting personal accounts in order to network for their personal reasons. Within organizations, e-mail has become an effective networking tool for employee groups, product teams, and overall intra-company communication.

Because e-mail provides a written record and an automatic time-stamp for information, it is more efficient than telephone for many communication transactions. You can send a single e-mail message to a distribution list of thousands with a single keystroke. You can also take an e-mail message and forward it to others. You can attach already prepared files, graphics, audio, and video to an e-mail message, and it will be correctly interpreted as long as the other person has a compatible e-mail program and the application needed to run the file.

Convenient, immediate, and paperless e-mail has made interpersonal communication inexpensive and efficient.

Anatomy of a Mail Message

Mail messages have two major parts: identifying information and the text message itself. The identifying information always includes the following:

To:

From:

Subject:

Date and Time:

Most e-mail programs allow you to send a message to an individual or to a distribution list. The e-mail program automatically completes the "From" field and the date and time. Here is a mail message screen waiting to be completed:

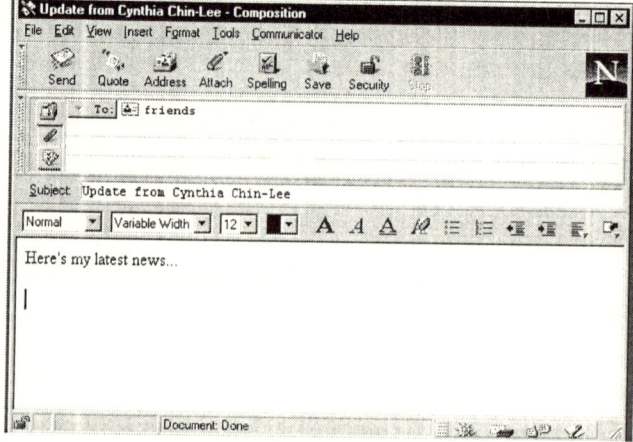

You generally have forty characters or less to give a subject heading to your message. Because e-mail users often get many messages per day (some of my friends receive hundreds of mail messages a day and keep over a thousand in their e-mail in-box), be sure to write an informative subject line. Don't leave the subject blank and don't say something as general as "hello" unless you're sure the recipient can tell who you are by your e-mail address.

It's better to write a subject that gives the receiver an idea of what you're writing about: "Status of Vanessa Young's résumé" or "Scheduling informational interview with you" or "Widget 5.0 Product Review Meeting."

In addition to the standard identifying information in an e-mail message, you often have optional fields for cc: (carbon copy) or bcc: (blind carbon copy). You use the cc: field to send the mail message to other people. If you want to send the mail message without having the recipient be aware of the other recipients, you use the bcc: field.

There are many e-mail programs available with many different features; some even include sophisticated scheduling and groupware software. Read the user's manual for your particular e-mail system to take full advantage of its features.

Message

After you complete the identifying information, you can write your e-mail message in the text field. In some systems, you are limited to about fifteen pages of text. Despite this limit, experts recommend that you keep most of your e-mail messages much shorter, no longer than six screens full of text (or about three pages).

If you want to attach a file on your computer to your message, most e-mail systems allow you to click a field to specify the file name or browse through your computer file system and select the file. If you are sending your message and attachment beyond the private network of your school, company, or online server, or over the Internet, remember that the recipient may need to have a compatible e-mail system and the application in which you created the attachment in order to read it.

Privacy

Although you may create an e-mail message for a particular person and send it to that person only, the receiver can forward your message to others. Many people have personal e-mail accounts and use them for personal networking. If you use a company account to send personal messages or messages of a private and confidential nature, you may risk your job. Employers can and do discipline or fire employees for misuse of corporate resources, such as the telephone, fax, e-mail, and the World Wide Web.

In a memorable incident at a high-tech company, a woman accidentally attached an intimate love letter to a joke she was posting to a humor interest group. When the company management found out the nature of the communication, both the woman and her associate were let go.

If you currently have a job, but are looking outside your company for another job, seriously consider getting a personal e-mail account for your job-hunting messages. Keep in mind that your manager and your system administrator usually can access and read company e-mail. You would not want to use your current employer's time and company resources to find another position.

Job-hunting by e-mail is one of the fastest ways to get a résumé to a company. Many job seekers have their résumé in two formats: an attractive desktop-published format and a plain text electronic résumé. You can attach or copy-and-paste a text résumé to a mail message to get your résumé to a potential employer quickly.

Jack, a technical writer, found one of his jobs by sending his text résumé by e-mail. Jack notes that "pretty" desktop-published résumés are nice, but, "Graphic design issues are not a primary concern to hiring managers; however, a well-organized résumé illustrates the organization of your thoughts."

Distribution Lists and Listservs

One of the best ways to network through e-mail is to send periodic updates to close friends and associates. Let your network of "A" contacts, the people you know well, find out what is new in your life with an e-mail update. Do not send an e-mail update to casual acquaintances (the "B" contact, the friend of the friend, or the "C" contacts, the distant acquaintance), because these casual acquaintances may feel your message is junk e-mail.

Every Christmas, I send out Christmas cards the old-fashioned way with cards, letters, return address labels, folding, sealing, and stamps. This is an annual ritual that is time-consuming and tedious, but important to me and my family. In contrast, every three months, I update my close contacts through e-mail. This is far less time-consuming than the annual Christmas card and a lot less costly. I keep a distribution list of the e-mail addresses of my "A" contacts in a file. In some systems, you can simply point to the file, which contains the list of names, and your message is sent to all the names in the file.

Here is a sample e-mail update that I sent out:

Subject: Update from Cynthia Chin-Lee
Hi, friends and family,
    I've been keeping my fingers busy typing at the keyboard these past few months. If you're interested in any of the following freelance articles, send me an e-mail message with your name and complete mailing address. Let me know if you want the article by e-mail or snail mail (U.S. mail):
In *High Technology Careers Magazine:*
    1. Informational Interviewing (includes quotes from good friend Gary Staas)
    2. Hitchhiking the Internet with Mosaic (co-authored with Comet).
New Children's Book
    I'm delighted to announce my next children's book, *A is for Asia,* will be published by Orchard Books of New York. The book is an alphabet book and a multicultural book with each letter of the alphabet describing a tradition, food, or animal from Asia. The illustrator will be Yumi Heo, an artist in New York with several publishing credits.
New Event
    You and your friends are invited to a Media Career Panel: Freelance Writers
Saturday, Dec. 10, 199x 11:00 am - 1:00 pm
Panelists: Cynthia Chin-Lee, Wendy Lichtman, Robin Stevens, Isobel Whits
Media Alliance, 814 Mission Street, Suite 205, San Francisco, CA 94103
To register with VISA or MasterCard call: (415) xxx-xxxx
$10 Media Alliance & MACMAG (non-profit) members, $15 non-members
Register Early – Registration is first come, first served!

That's it! Andy and Vanessa say hello.
Sincerely,
Cyndi
The Networking Queen
Author of *It's Who You Know, Almond Cookies and Dragon Well Tea,* and *A Is for Asia.*
Web site:
http://www.expertcenter.com/members/cchinlee

Your e-mail update could include your major accomplishments at work or at home, major vacations, how your children are doing, news on your hobbies, or sharing your goals.

Signatures

At the end of the update, you might want to include your e-mail signature, like the one shown above. The e-mail signature is a file that is automatically appended to every mail message you send. Like a business card, it provides information that you want to provide. Many people include all or some of the following in their e-mail signature:
Address (home or business)
Phone numbers (fax and voice)
E-mail address and web site address
Hobbies or favorite quote

The Language of Emoticons

Because mail messages are generally text only, you can't hear the inflection in someone's communication as you read. E-mail users have developed "emoticons," also called "smileys," to express emotions to accentuate the feelings behind their messages. These are read sideways and include the following samples:

    :-)   Smile
    ;-)   Winking smile.
    :-(Frown.
    :-o   Wow
    :-*   Oops
    8-O   "Omigod!!"

You may also use abbreviations in your e-mail, such as, IMHO (in my humble opinion), BTW (by the way), and TTFN (ta ta for now).

Listservs: E-mail Distribution Lists

Besides the information networking you can do by sending e-mail messages to key contacts and friends, you can network through e-mail listservs. A listserv is a distribution list of e-mail addresses for people who are members of an organization, such as a professional society, or who are interested in a particular topic. Professional organizations are one of the most fertile grounds for networking for your career and many of them have listservs for their members.

For example, the San Francisco chapter of the Society for Technical Communication, a professional organization for technical writers, editors, and illustrators, has a listserv for its members interested in current job openings. If you send an e-mail message to the listserv address, the software adds your name to the distribution list and you automatically receive weekly e-mail messages that list the current full-time and contract job openings. Even if you're not looking for a job, this is still a smart way to see the employment activity in the area.

Another professional society, the Society of Children's Book Writers and Illustrators has a national listserv for members. The SCBWI listserv sends out messages periodically announcing professional conferences, events, and news of interest to its members. Both of the above listservs are moderated, meaning that a person or team controls what is distributed by e-mail to all members of the listserv. Moderated listservs help prevent a member from sending inappropriate materials, "flames," or unsolicited promotions.

In contrast to moderated listservs, there are also many listservs that are unmoderated. If you join an unmoderated listserv, anyone can send a message to the listserv address and every member of the listserv will receive the message. Many unmoderated listservs have a high volume of e-mail messages and, if you join one, you may find your e-mail in-box inundated daily.

To find a listserv to match your interests, ask your professional group if it has one. You also can search for a listserv on the Internet; many listservs are advertised on web sites. Here are two web sites dedicated to listing listservs:

http://www.NeoSoft.com/internet/paml/byname.html
http://cuisung.unige.ch/eao/www/Internet/Listserv.txt

Usenet News

Usenet news is an electronic bulletin board system (BBS) that is devoted to the discussion of specific topics. Unlike listservs, where the mail message from the listserv comes directly to your e-mail in-box, with Usenet news, you must use a Usenet news reader to read the messages, also called articles, posted to a news group. Most Internet service providers will provide a Usenet news reader as well as e-mail and a web browser as part of their service, but you may need to ask for it. Usenet articles are similar in format to e-mail messages, and posting one is similar to sending an e-mail message except you use a Usenet news program, rather than your e-mail program.

There are 20,000-plus news groups on a wide variety of subjects, including social issues, religion, soap operas, job listings, career topics, and so on.

News groups follow a naming convention according to the topic:

rec. news groups are geared to humor, arts, hobbies, and recreation.

alt. news groups are "alternative" groups for weirder topics and the offbeat.

biz. news groups are business groups where product announcements, reviews, and marketing materials can be posted.

comp. news groups are for computer-related topics, including hardware and software.

news. news groups talk about the Usenet network itself.

misc. news groups discuss subjects not easily classified.

For example, misc.jobs.misc is a national news group for discussing job-related issues. And ba.misc.jobs. is a news group for discussing job-related issues in the San Francisco Bay Area. There are news groups that are regionally oriented and they often include the regional abbreviation at the end of the news group name. For example, you can find job listings for Toronto in tor.jobs, jobs in Colorado at co.jobs, and jobs in Pittsburgh at pgh.jobs. Clerical jobs in Portland are listed in pdax.jobs.clerical and volunteer jobs are listed in pdaxs.jobs.volunteers.

You can post your résumé to advertise your availability on misc.jobs.résumés. If you're interested in jobs only in the Bay Area, you'd post it at ba.jobs.résumés. Although many jobs listed and found on the Internet are still computer-related, more and more industries are using the Internet as a job recruitment tool. If you're in biotechnology, for example, there is a news group called bionet.jobs.offered and a related news group called bionet.jobs.wanted. If you're looking for a business job, you might try the business-oriented news group, biz.jobs.offered. And if you're just starting out, misc.jobs.offered.entry may have some good possibilities.

If you're interested in getting opinions or personal anecdotes on just about any topic, you'll find Usenet news is a great place. Many people meet via Usenet news groups because they can discuss the topics they are interested in. One recent acquaintance told me how he met his girlfriend on a business spirituality news group. Mark says, "Relationships can develop naturally. We got to know each other first without worrying about physical appearances."

Usenet news archives are a wonderful resource for looking up commonly asked questions on many topics from personal finance to the best breadmaker. To look at an index of archived news, go to this web site:

http://www.dejanews.com

You can also look at the following news groups to get a list of listservs that you may want to join:

news.answers
news.lists

7

Finding Career Resources on the World Wide Web

The Web is a vast ocean of knowledge, hobbies, ideas, and topics of special interest. The daily discovery of new things stimulates the mind and expands horizons, unlike TV, which generally has the opposite effect.

— David M. Chandler
author, Running a Perfect Web Site

The World Wide Web is only a subset of the Internet, but it is one of the most exciting and interesting parts of it. Web sites are files, usually with text and graphics, that are voluntarily hosted on computers and made publicly accessible on the Internet. Some web sites are complex with animation, video, audio, and programs that can draw maps or fetch information from databases.

Companies, schools, and individuals create web sites and share their information for free on the Web. To be part of the World Wide Web, web sites must follow the hypertext transfer protocol (HTTP) and be written in hypertext markup language (HTML). What distinguishes the Web from other parts of the Internet is its easy-to-use, point-and-click interface. Here is an example of my web site:

A web site is a series of pages, and the first page is called the home page. The terms web site and home page are often used interchangeably. To access a web site, you need to have the address.

Enter the web site address into a program called a web browser, such as Netscape or Microsoft Explorer. In seconds (or minutes, depending on the speed of the Internet connection and the size of the web page), the web page appears on your computer screen. You can scroll through the web page, print it, and even save the page to a file on your own computer. Web pages include underlined text, called a hypertext link, that you can click to move to another web page. The target web page can be part of the same web site or a page on another web site in another part of the world, created and hosted by some other person or organization.

An address for a web site is also called a uniform resource locator or URL. URLs for web sites always start with "http://."

The http stands for hypertext transfer protocol because all web sites use this computer protocol. Many web sites have the letters www (standing for World Wide Web) in their URLs, but it's not required. Web site URLs, like e-mail addresses in a domain, must be unique.

Let's examine a web site address:
http://www.expertcenter.com/members/cchinlee/

In this URL, the http:// shows the resource type (hypertext transfer protocol). Other resource types would be FTP (file transfer protocol), or Gopher.

Following the slashes is the domain name: www.expertcenter.com

Following the domain name is a pointer to a directory name (members) and then a pointer to the file name for my web site (cchinlee).

Setting up a Web Site

The Expert Center is the company I pay to host my web site. If you want a web site, you can pay a company or your Internet service provider to host it. If you're ambitious, you can set up one yourself. Many books and web sites explain how to set up a web server to host your web site. Chapter 8 explains how to create a simple web site, but you will still need to do additional work to connect the web site to the World Wide Web.

Searching the Web

The World Wide Web has rich resources for career and personal interests; however, you have to do some digging to find what you want. Even if you don't find what you want today, remember that web site creators continually update their sites, and thousands of new sites are added to the Web every month.

When you launch a web browser, a web page automatically appears. The web page that appears may be the home page for the company that created the web browser (for example, the Netscape web site), or it may be the web site for the organization that owns the computer (the public library, your company, or your online service). Often this home page will have a search field in which you can enter a keyword or a series of keywords to conduct the search.

To begin a search, enter your keywords and press Return (or click on Submit); the search engine will start searching the World Wide Web for web sites that contain the keywords you entered. Each search engine has a set of rules that dictate how it will search for web sites that contain your keywords.

What can you find on the Web? If you don't have a definite topic in mind, look at sites designed for the groups that you belong to, your profession, or your hobbies. There are sites for women, men, minorities, gays, and the disabled. You will find web sites for professionals, such as engineers, writers, artists, journalists, doctors, law enforcement, teachers, scientists, marketing, advertising, and more. You can also locate web sites for cities, geographic regions, schools and for popular interests, such as the stock market, sports, literature, religion, and music.

Boolean Searches

To narrow down the web sites for viewing, you may want to brush up on Boolean logic. Many search engines use Boolean logic to determine which web sites meet your criteria. You'll need to read the rules associated with the search engine on the home page to understand the best ways to enter keywords. To find these rules, there is often a button called Help that will explain the rules.

If you've never studied Boolean logic, here are a few hints.

1. You can search for keywords in a specific order by surrounding the keywords in quote marks. For example, you want to search on San Francisco, type "San Francisco," making sure to enclose the words in quotation marks (""). Then you won't find web sites that include the words "John Francisco" or "San Anselmo."

2. You can show relationships with operators, such as AND, OR, NOT. If you want to search for San Francisco law schools, you might type "San Francisco" AND "law schools" to find information on law schools in San Francisco.

If you want to find law schools in San Francisco and Washington, D.C., you would enter "law schools" AND "San Francisco" OR "Washington, D.C."

If you want information on vegetables, but not carrots, you would enter "vegetable" AND NOT "carrot."

3. To find information on a person, you might enter the first name and the last name connected by the operator NEAR. By using NEAR, you'll find sites that have the two words within, say, ten words of each other. To find information on Charles Dickens, you would enter Charles NEAR Dickens.

This way, you will find web sites on Charles Dickens even if the web site has listed the name as Dickens, Charles.

Popular Search Engines and Search Directories

The World Wide Web has many web sites that specialize in searching the web. Most of these sites use a search engine, a program that has an algorithm for find the web sites. My personal favorite is http://www.altavista. digital.com because of its speed, advanced search tools, and its ability to search the World Wide Web as well as Usenet news.

Note: All web addresses were verified at the time of production. However, realize that web addresses change and web sites come and go.

There are also web sites are that are directories, which have the advantage of having a person who reads and categorizes the web sites. For example, Yahoo! (http://www.yahoo.com) is a directory that has a web librarian, who looks at each web site and decides how to categorize it.

Some web sites, like http://www.mckinley.com, also rate the quality of sites with a zero to five-star rating or will give a "green light" to sites that they consider appropriate for general viewing.

Some popular web sites that specialize in web searches are as follows:

    http://www.altavista.digital.com
    http://www.lycos.com
    http://www.webcrawler.com
    http://www.excite.com
    http://guide.infoseek.com
    http://www.mckinley.com/
    http://www.hotbot.com

http://www.search.com
http://www.yahoo.com

Or, you might try one of these web sites that boast access to multiple search engines:

http://www.all4one.com (searches AltaVista, Lycos, Yahoo, Webcrawler)

http://wagner.cs.colostate.edu:1969/ (20 search engines)

Career Web Sites

If you're looking for work or thinking about changing careers, you'll find a wealth of career resources, including career magazine, job fairs, and recruiters on the Web. If you've targeted certain industries or a company, you'll also often find a web site for your industry or target company. For example, the Society for Technical Communication (Silicon Valley) hosts a web site that has job listings (http://stc.org/region8/svc/www). The job listings include job descriptions, salary ranges, and e-mail links to hiring managers.

If you want to work for a large company, chances are you can view its web site for product information, corporate profiles, maps to company locations, stock information, and more specifically, its job postings. You can sometimes guess the corporate web site address because many companies are listed as www.companyname.com. For instance, Intuit, a software maker, is http://www.intuit.com; Pacific Gas and Electric, a utility, (PG&E) is http://www.pge.com.

Job Fairs

If you have looked for a job, you may have attended a job fair — a chaotic hall filled with booths from various companies, staffed with recruiters and hiring managers pitching their companies. On the Internet, you will find the online equivalent. Most web sites that host job fairs are magazines, recruiters, and job fair companies.

The Virtual Job Fair (http://www.vjf.com), for example, is run by an organization that runs real job fairs in San Jose, California. It has several sections in its web site: Westech Career Expo, Job Search, High Technology Careers (an online magazine), Résumé Center, Library and Career Resources, Virtual Job Fair, and Human Resource Center. The Job Search lists more than 500 companies and 15,000 positions. The Library and Resource Center has employment databases from daily newspapers all over the United States and also includes employment databases in Africa, Asia, Australia and New Zealand, Canada, Europe, Mexico and South America, the Middle East, and Scandinavia. Another popular area for career information is on Yahoo!. Look at http://www.yahoo.com/Business_and_Economy/ Companies/Career_and_Job_Search_Services/ for web sites on planning and coaching, résumé and job banks (thousands of sites), and training.

E-span (http://www.espan.com) is another site to check for its Job Search section. Here you can search for a job by keyword or to fit your qualifications. E-span's site also features Career Companion with 6,000 resources for professionals, and HR Professional, with resources especially for human resources professionals. Similar job fair sites include CareerMosaic (http://www.careermosaic.com), an international gateway listing positions in Thailand and Singapore. and the Monster Board (http://www.monster.com), with sections for both job-seekers and corporate recruiters.

Small Business Sites

If you're an entrepreneur, you'll probably want to look at the Small Business Administration web site at http://www.sba.gov. For small business tax information and downloadable tax forms, go straight to the IRS at http://www.irs.ustreas.gov.

Other Interesting Career Web Sites

Here are some other web sites that are networking or career-related that you'll find interesting. If you are searching for a career that matches your personality, try the set of career quizzes at:

http://www.aboutwork.com/resourcecenter.

Once you have found the appropriate choices of careers, you can do some online investigation of these careers at a web site sponsored by the Bureau of Labor Statistics. The web site, http://stats.bls.gov/ocohome.htm, hosts an online version of the *Occupational Outlook Handbook* and describes the major professions, requirements, and growth of the profession.

Finally, if you want to find a long lost friend who might be on the Internet, you can use one of the white page listings on the web. My favorite white pages listing is at Bigfoot (http://www.bigfoot.com). Alternatively, to make new online contacts, you can register for online networking at the web site Sixdegrees (http://www.sixdegrees.com). The "six degrees" comes from the playwright John Guare who wrote that "everyone on earth is connected ot everyone else through a path of six people or less." What a great networking concept!

8

Creating a Simple Web Site

> *I hope that the Internet becomes a deliriously fun, gigantic swap meet of cultural riches open to everyone on Earth, without barriers, and that it maintains it anarchic character.*
> — *Jaron Lanier*

If you want to create your own web site, this chapter should get you started. Depending on how computer literate you already are, you may want to invest in a book, class, or a consultant to create your web site. If this technical stuff makes you feel squeamish, skip the chapter and read Chapter Nine, Maximizing Your Networking.

How It Works

To create a web page, you'll need a word processor or editor that can create a text (ASCII) file. The Macintosh operating system contains an editor called SimpleText, and the Windows operating system comes with an editor called Notepad.

You'll use mark-up codes like <P> for paragraph and <H1> for a first-level heading to mark up your text. You'll save your file with a file name with the extension .html (for Macintosh or Unix computers) or .htm (for PCs). You can view how your page will look on the Internet by starting your web browser and entering a URL that points to the local file system:

file://localhost/C:/directory/file-name

PC users would indicate their hard disk by C: or D: or whatever their drive is named, for example:

file://localhost/C:/mypage.htm

A Macintosh user would enter the name of his disk (rather than a letter), such as:

file://localhost/MacDisk/mypage.html

Once you create your web site, you will need to have it hosted on the Internet. You can pay a company or your Internet service provider to host it, or set up your own web server. Explaining how to set up a web server goes beyond the scope of this book, but there are many books, magazine articles, and web sites that show you how to do it.

Easy HTML

First let's learn some HTML. In this example, you'll use four HTML elements, called tags: HTML, HEAD, TITLE, BODY. All web pages start and end with the HTML tag. The start HTML tag is <HTML> and the ending tag is </HTML>. Within these tags are the two main parts of a page: the head <HEAD> and the body <BODY>. The head contains the title <TITLE> of the page and the body contains the contents of the page.

Create a file in an editor that includes these lines:

```
<HTML>
<HEAD>
<TITLE>
```

Creating a Simple Web Site

```
My Home Page
</TITLE>
</HEAD>
<BODY>
Put whatever text you want here.
</BODY>
</HTML>
```

Save the file. You may want to create a directory or folder called "web" and save the file in that directory/folder. Or you could save the file at the desktop level so you can find it easily. You must save the file with the extension .HTML or .HTM (for example, mypage.html or mypage.htm). The file type must be text (the default).

To view your simple web page, start your browser and enter the file name of your web page. Instead of using http:// to show a web page on the Internet, use the following to specify a file on the local file system:

file://localhost/C:/web/mypage.htm

If your file doesn't look right or isn't viewable, check to make sure you didn't misspell any tags. Because it's sometimes hard to check your own spelling, ask a friend to look it over if you get frustrated.

More HTML Tags

Open the file you created above and add some content between the start <BODY> tag and the ending </BODY> tag. The following example includes the first-level heading tag <H1>, the paragraph tag <P>, the second-level heading tag <H2>, and the third-level heading tag <H3>.

```
<BODY>
<H1>
About Me
</H1>
<P>
```

```
Write something here about yourself.
</P>
<H2>
My Career Goals
</H2>
<P>
Write something here about your goals.
</P>
<H3>
My Hobbies
</H3>
<P>
Write something about your hobbies.
</P>
</BODY>
```

Save the file and look at it in your browser. Here is an example of the HTML used to make my web site on page 138.

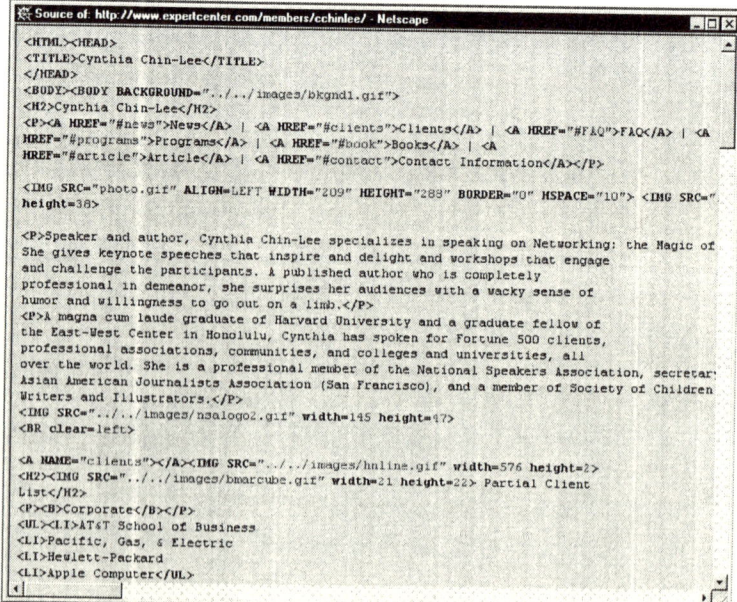

List Tags and More

Now that you've learned the basic tags, you can start making your web page a little fancier with the list tags. <UL> is the unordered list tag which means the beginning of a bulleted list. <LI> indicates a list item. Note that the end list item tag </LI> is optional.

You can format your text to make it bold <B> or emphasized <EM>. Remember these tags require ending tags </B> and </EM>.

Open your file and add the following tags and text:

```
<P>
This is a list of my favorite things:
<UL>
<LI>
Apple strudel
<LI>
Ice cream
<LI>
Hawaii
<LI>
You fill in whatever you like
</UL>
<P>
I would like everyone to know this:
<B>
Fill in something very important here!
</B>
</P>
<P>
If I knew this twenty years ago, it would have saved me a lot of time and effort:
<EM>
Fill in your piece of wisdom here.
</EM>
</P>
```

Save the file and look at it in your browser.

Creating a HyperText Link Within a Page

Now you're ready to create a hypertext link. Remember a link appears on a page as underlined text. When you click on the link, you will jump to another location (either on the same page, another page in the same web site, or another location in an entirely different web site which could exist on another computer in another country!). To create a hypertext link, you use an anchor tag and a destination tag.

The anchor tag has two parts. The first part of the anchor tag (in bold) indicates where the link should jump to. In this case, the tag specifies that the link jumps to a place called Values.

`<A HREF="#Values">Values</A>`

The second part of the anchor tag (in bold) specifies the text that will be underlined. In this case, the word "My Values" will be underlined:

`<A HREF="#Values">My Values</A>`

The destination tag is the location where the link will jump:

`<A NAME="Values">`

Open your file and edit it to include the following text in the body:

```
<P>
Here is my first hypertext link.
</P>
<A HREF="#Values">My Values</A>
<P>
Type in some stuff here. Type in about 100 words or more. This way you can really see something happen with the links above.
<P>
Type in some stuff here. Type in about 100 words or more. This way you can really see something happen with the links above.
```

```
<A NAME="Values">
<P>
I consider my most important values to be
family, friends, community, education and self-
development.
```

Save the file and look at it in your browser. You should see the words "My Values" underlined. When you click on the underlined word, the link should jump to the paragraph where you entered your values.

Other HTML Tags

There are many other HTML tags for more advanced formatting. Such tags include tables, frames, graphics, and so on. For a complete list of HTML 3.2 tags, see Appendix A.

Creating a HyperText Link to Another File

Most web sites contain more than one page. You can create a link to another web page using the anchor tag. First create a second page to link to. Call the page "second.htm" and include the following:

```
<HTML>
<HEAD>
<TITLE>
My second page
</TITLE>
</HEAD>
<BODY>
<P>
This is my second file.
</BODY>
</HTML>
```

Save this file.

In your first file add the following anchor within the body of the page:

`<A HREF="file://localhost/C:/web/second.htm">Second file</A>`

Save the first file. Now open your browser and look at your first file. Click on the link to the second page. The link should jump to your second file.

See Appendix A for a list of HTML tags and Appendix B for a sample web site.

9

Maximizing Your Networking

Networking has enormous potential to help you achieve your career and personal goals. According to Venda Raye-Johnson, author of *Effective Networking*, "the greatest leadership skill is the networking skill." You can maximize your networking efforts by increasing your visibility and improving your self-image. To increase your visibility, you need to extend your personal contacts through meeting people outside your normal network of personal contacts. To improve your self-image, you must objectively review your appearance and communication skills.

The following opportunities will help to increase your contacts:

- Teaching.
- Public speaking.
- Consulting.
- Publishing articles and books.
- Becoming a leader in a volunteer organization.

- Competing in your field or running for public office.
- Networking on the Internet.

Teaching

You can increase your visibility by teaching, either full- or part-time. If you have worked several years in a particular field, but do not have a teaching credential or an education background, you may still qualify to instruct in the area of your expertise. Many people successfully transfer their experience in industry to the classroom and expand their contacts at the same time.

For example, Hari left his position as an engineer for an aerospace company to become a full-time professor at the University of California. In addition to the respect he has gained as a professor, he supervises bright graduate students, does research in his field, and enjoys a flexible schedule that allows him to conduct highly-paid consulting work for an international satellite conglomerate. Hari may remain a teacher for a number of years, or he can return to industry. He is in an excellent position because teaching has enhanced his reputation and has given him more freedom to pursue other interests.

Not all of us want to teach full time, but many can take advantage of part-time teaching positions. There are opportunities to teach at junior colleges or adult education programs in the evening. By teaching, you increase contacts by building relationships with the college administration, faculty, and students. Teaching also helps to create name recognition in your field. My mentor, for example, taught for several years at the local extension school. He says, "I enjoyed teaching because it helped others. But it has also helped my business a lot. After I started my own company, some of my students came to seek my expertise and hired my firm as their consultant."

Public Speaking

If a teaching job sounds like too large of a commitment, one-time or short-term public speaking may be more suitable. You can volunteer to give seminars or speeches at work or through other avenues. For example, you might speak at career fairs, panels at local colleges, or a program for your professional or community organization. You can sign up for a speaker's bureau or join a speaking club, such as the National Speaker's Association or Toastmasters International. Both of these organizations provide many opportunities to speak and become more visible. If people in your audience like what you say and how you say it, they could contact you for a new and exciting opportunity.

Consulting

Like teaching and public speaking, consulting full-time or part-time can give you more chances to hear about opportunities in your field. Donna, a massage therapist, had some career setbacks and was anxious to find work. She sent more than twenty-five letters and résumés to massage businesses, chiropractic offices, and physical therapy practices, but only one person called to arrange an interview. She recounts:

> I was feeling discouraged when a recently graduated massage practitioner came to me for consulting. In our conversation, she mentioned a massage therapist position

at her company that she eventually decided not to take. I then asked if she would mind if I applied for the massage job. I applied for the position and was hired. If she had not come to consult with me, I would not have been aware of the opening. This is just one of various experiences in my life in which I felt helped by some invisible guidance at a time when I needed something and was open to change.

Publishing Articles and Books

Contributing articles to the company newsletter, the local papers or regional magazines, or publishing a book can also increase your visibility and help make contacts. Published authors enjoy a certain aura of respect. My friend Wanda works full-time as a public affairs specialist at a corporation, but she frequently writes in her spare time. Like many people, her life has many facets, and each of these facets, including writing, has worked together to make up a varied and full career:

> I have worked as a communicator, writer, and a teacher. I have been involved with athletics, particularly swimming on an international level. I have also worked with literacy programs. One of the interesting and rewarding aspects of networking is how these have interconnected to my benefit. An article I wrote for a swimming magazine led to another writing assignment on business. When I made a 3,000-mile relocation, my swimming contacts assured me of a job at my destination. Other swimming contacts allowed me to make a career change from teacher to full-time communicator. And through a professional organization, I was approached to do public relations for several athletic events.

Becoming a Leader of a Volunteer Organization

Volunteer for task forces, committees, or club activities where you work or where you live. Becoming a leader through a voluntary organization gives you a chance to practice management skills while increasing your visibility in the organization and community. Dave, a technical training specialist, has volunteer work as his hobby. A runner himself, Dave helps other American runners learn about the Soviet Union through international running events. He also is active in a company speaking club and in a mentor program for less privileged high school students. Says Dave, "The people who I have met through my community work have enriched my life and in some cases have proven to be useful contacts."

Volunteer work can give far more benefits than imagined. According to a 1988 study at the University of Michigan Survey Research Center, regular volunteer work, more than any other activity, dramatically increases life expectancy. The study tracked 2,700 people for ten years to determine the impact of social relationships on health. The results were especially clear for men. Men who did not volunteer were two and one-half times more likely to die during the study period than those who volunteered at least once a week.

Competing in Your Field or Running for Public Office

Most fields hold competitions for excellence; these contests could be academic, literary, or athletic. By competing in your field, you can increase your reputation and visibility. If you win the competition, you earn even greater respect from your peers.

Likewise, you can run for public office to serve your community or your local, state, or national government. By becoming active in local or national politics, you advance your name in greater and greater circles of recognition, and you can help ensure that government is being run fairly and competently.

Improving Your Self-Image

Besides increasing your visibility, you maximize your networking opportunities by enhancing your self-image. How do you appear to people? Ask yourself questions about your style and demeanor — specifically: your appearance, hairstyle, attire, voice, eye contact, and posture. Some people have almost everything: intelligence, education, and even great networking skills, yet they lack a proper self-image, one that projects professionalism. Read books about building a strong personal image or seek a professional image consultant if help is needed in this area.

In addition to working on outward appearance, analyze your communication skills. Take classes in public speaking, listening skills, diction, or accent improvement. Join a speaker's club to learn how others perceive you. Have yourself videotaped or audiotaped while in practice interview situations or while giving a brief talk. Be as objective as possible when looking for areas where you could improve. As difficult as it may be to change, take the steps needed to improve your image. You could be pleasantly surprised by the positive responses received from the people around you.

Networking on the Internet

Technology offers a host of resources that did not exist a few years ago. You can dramatically increase your networking effectiveness by using the tools available now. In addition to the telephone and fax machine, take advantage of your personal database or software designed to manage personal contacts. Such programs can help you create an address book, print mailing labels, or even dial your phone. These programs often have note fields for recording information on the personal contact as well as scheduling software to remind you to stay in touch with key contacts.

You can use Internet applications, such as e-mail, listservs, and the World Wide Web, to enlarge your area of knowledge and communication. Take the example of Christina, a technical editor. She and 600 coworkers were laid off in a corporate downsizing. As a twenty-something single woman, who networked frequently in her profession, Christina turned to her e-mail contacts for some professional leads. One of her acquaintances, Roger, a former contractor at her company, had kept in contact with one of his former colleagues from another company. Roger's former colleague now lived in another town, but he had heard of an editing position at an expanding company in the area where Roger and Christina lived. Aware that Christina had been laid off and was looking for a job, Roger forwarded the e-mail message about the open position to Christina. Christina followed up and successfully landed the position.

When Jill was searching for a job, she didn't have to go any farther than the computer. She used the virtual job fair at http://www.vjf.com to submit résumés to thirty companies. Said Jill, "With just my résumé, they're flying me 2,000 miles to interview with several different departments." Jill not only interviewed for several jobs, she also "got a job offer and accepted it!"

James is another networking convert. He used the Monster Board (http://www.monster.com) to find his job. He writes, "Before I gave it a try, I wasn't sure if the jobs you posted were for real. Now I know that they are because I just got a sweet job with Time Inc./New Media."

A Networking Story: Who Will Get the Promotion?

Counselor and author Dr. Judith Pearson describes two qualified people competing for the same management position within their company. They each will be interviewed for the promotion by the corporate vice president. What are each of their strategies for obtaining this highly sought-after position?

Joe goes for a beer with some friends after work and announces that he is in the running for the promotion. His friends rally around, but none of them knows how to help; Joe does not know how to get help himself.

On the other hand, Julie knows how to network and get help. She calls three co-workers who can help her get through the job interview effectively. She invites each of them to lunch separately to help prepare for the interview. Her first colleague, Cathy, holds a job that is roughly equivalent to the one for which Julie is applying. Cathy can tell her what the job requires, the problems she might encounter and the strategies she can use to solve them. Her second colleague, Chuck, plays golf with the vice president and gives Julie some ideas as to what might impress him, some of his likes and dislikes, what his personal interests are, and whether or not he is family-oriented. Jane is Julie's close friend, and they will practice interviewing. Jane will critique Julie's interviewing skills.

Who do you think will be better prepared to get the promotion at the interview with the vice president?

A Final Note

As you use your network to accomplish goals, keep a positive attitude. Don't be discouraged by the naysayers. A person with a negative attitude can transform almost any situation, no matter how initially bright and promising, into a dark and hopeless abyss. When you tell a naysayer that you are considering a move from Los Angeles to Des Moines, he will point out all the reasons why you should not do it (you may miss the sophisticated city attractions and the cultural diversity), and he will overlook the reasons why you would want to move (such as the slower pace and lower cost of living). On the other hand, if you were to move from Des Moines to Los Angeles, another naysayer would tell you that you cannot afford the high rents and you will hate the smog.

You will encounter many naysayers in the job market. If you have a masters in economics, but no work experience, and apply for a job as a business analyst, the naysayer will tell you that you don't qualify because you are underexperienced. Conversely, if you have ten years of experience as a business analyst, but no college degree, the same person would inform you that you are overexperienced, but undereducated.

Discount the naysayers and surround yourself with optimistic, high-esteem people. Len Sandler writes in *Training Magazine,* "The simple truth is that almost all of us behave pretty much according to the way we're treated." In the late 1950s, Columbia sociology professor Robert Merton conceptualized the "self-fulfilling prophecy." Merton said that once you set an expectation, even if it is not accurate, you tend to act in ways that are consistent with that expectation. The result is that the expectation becomes reality, as if by magic. If your own expectations, and those of the people around you, are failure and mediocrity, then that is what you will probably get. On the other hand, if your expectation is to achieve your goals, and you are buoyed by the confidence and praise of those around you, you will most likely succeed. The magic in these results is not voodoo; the magic is simply in your positive and unswaying attitude.

Summary

Is your net working? Concentrate on the positive contacts in your network, and you will find yourself going places. Your network can help if you are laid off or fired, if you want a promotion or a career change, or even if you are trying to meet routine needs, such as finding a place to live or a new dentist. As you become successful at networking, help others build their networks, too.

Meeting people, helping them, and letting them help you, will enrich your life immensely. Get ready for new challenges and the excitement of realizing your dreams. Maximize your networking opportunities by enhancing your self-image and by expanding your normal circle of contacts through opportunities, such as leading a volunteer organization, or through public speaking. Networking takes ability, timing, trust, and team work; it is a demanding art, but one that allows greater control of your future.

With our volatile economy and the highly competitive international marketplace, you cannot afford to leave your fate to others. Use your network as a safety net. If you should ever trip on the high wire of life, your personal network will ensure you get a soft landing and that you bounce back to even greater heights.

Appendix A: HTML 3.2 Tags

HTML Elements in Alphabetic Order

Element	Element Type	Attributes
`<!>`	Doc. Structure	None
`<A>`	Special	HREF
		NAME
		REL
		REV
		TITLE
`<ADDRESS>`	Body	None
`<APPLET>`	Special	ALIGN
		ALT
		CODE
		CODEBASE
		HEIGHT
		HSPACE
		NAME
		VSPACE
		WIDTH
`<AREA>`	Client-Side Map	ALT

		COORDS
		HREF
		NOHREF
		SHAPE
<B>	Font	None
<BASE>	Head	HREF
<BIG>	Font	None
<BLOCKQUOTE>	Body	None
<BODY>	Doc. Struc.	ALINK
		BACKGROUND
		BGCOLOR
		LINK
		TEXT
		VLINK
 	Special	CLEAR
<CAPTION>	Table	ALIGN
<CENTER>	Body	None
<CITE>	Phrase	None
<CODE>	Phrase	None
<DD>	List	None
<DFN>	Phrase	None
<DIR>	List	COMPACT
<DIV>	Body	ALIGN
<DL>	List	COMPACT
<DT>	List	None
<EM>	Phrase	None
<FONT>	Special	COLOR
		FACE
		SIZE
<FORM>	Form	ACTION
		ENCTYPE
		METHOD
<FRAMES>	Frame	MARGINHEIGHT
		MARGINWIDTH
		NAME
		NORESIZE
		SCROLLING
		SRC
FRAMESET	Frame	COLS
		ROWS
<H1>...<H6>	Body	ALIGN
<HEAD>	Doc. Struc.	None

Appendix A

Tag	Category	Attributes
<HR>	Body	ALIGN
		NOSHADE
		SIZE
		WIDTH
<HTML>	Doc. Struc.	version.attr
<I>	Font	None
<IMG>	Special	ALIGN
		ALT
		BORDER
		HEIGHT
		HSPACE
		ISMAP
		SRC
		USEMAP
		VSPACE
		WIDTH
<INPUT>	Form	ALIGN
		CHECKED
		MAXLENGTH
		NAME
		PASSWORD
		RADIO
		RESET
		SIZE
		SRC
		SUBMIT
		TEXT
		TYPE
		VALUE
<ISINDEX>	Head	PROMPT
<KBD>	Phrase	None
<LH>	List	None
<LI>	List	TYPE
		VALUE
<LINK>	Head	HREF
		ID
		REL
		REV
		TITLE
<MAP>	Client-Side Map	NAME
<MENU>	List	COMPACT

Tag	Category	Attributes
`<META>`	Head	CONTENT
		HTTP-EQUIV
		NAME
`<NOFRAMES>`	Frame	None
`<OL>`	List	COMPACT
		TYPE
		START
`<OPTION>`	Form	SELECTED
		VALUE
`<P>`	Body	ALIGN
`<PARAM>`	Special	NAME
		VALUE
`<PLAINTEXT>`	Body	None
`<SAMP>`	Phrase	None
`<SCRIPT>`	Special	
`<SELECT>`	Form	MULTIPLE
		NAME
		SIZE
`<SMALL>`	Font	None
`<STRIKE>`	Font	None
`<STRONG>`	Phrase	None
`<STYLE>`	Head	
`<SUB>`	Font	None
`<SUP>`	Font	None
`<TABLE>`	Table	ALIGN
		BORDER
		CELLSPACING
		CELLPADDING
		WIDTH
`<TD>`	Table	COLSPAN
		ROWSPAN
		NOWRAP
		cell.HALIGN
		cell.VALIGN
`<TEXTAREA>`	Form	COLS
		NAME
		ROWS
`<TEXTFLOW>`	Special	
`<TH>`	Table	COLSPAN
		ROWSPAN
		NOWRAP
		cell.HALIGN

Appendix A   171

		cell.VALIGN
<TITLE>	Head	None
<TR>	Table	cell.HALIGN
		cell.VALIGN
<TT>	Font	None
<UL>	List	COMPACT
		TYPE
<VAR>	Phrase	None

HTML Elements by Type

Document Structure   Elements

```
<!>
<BODY>              ALINK
                    BACKGROUND
                    BGCOLOR
                    LINK
                    TEXT
                    VLINK
<HEAD>
<HTML>              version.attr
```

Head   Elements

```
<BASE>              HREF
<ISINDEX>           PROMPT
<LINK>              HREF
                    ID
                    REL
                    REV
                    TITLE
<META>              CONTENT
                    HTTP-EQUIV
                    NAME
<SCRIPT>
<STYLE>
<TITLE>
```

Body   Elements

```
<ADDRESS>
<BLOCKQUOTE>
<CENTER>
<DIV>               ALIGN
<HR>                ALIGN
                    NOSHADE
                    SIZE
                    WIDTH
<H1>...<H6>         ALIGN
```

Appendix A 173

<P>   ALIGN
<PLAINTEXT>

Font Elements
<B>
<BIG>
<I>
<SMALL>
<STRIKE>
<SUB>
<SUP>
<TT>

Phrase Elements
<CITE>
<CODE>
<DFN>
<EM>
<KBD>
<SAMP>
<STRONG>
<VAR>

Special Elements
<A>   HREF
                         NAME
                         REL
                         REV
                         TITLE
<APPLET>   ALIGN
                         ALT
                         CODE
                         CODEBASE
                         HEIGHT
                         HSPACE
                         NAME
                         VSPACE
                         WIDTH

                  CLEAR
<FONT>   COLOR
                         FACE

`<IMG>`	SIZE
	ALIGN
	ALT
	BORDER
	HEIGHT
	HSPACE
	ISMAP
	SRC
	USEMAP
	VSPACE
	WIDTH
`<PARAM>`	NAME
	VALUE
`<SCRIPT>`	
`<TEXTFLOW>`	

Form Elements

`<FORM>`	ACTION
	ENCTYPE
	METHOD
`<INPUT>`	ALIGN
	CHECKED
	MAXLENGTH
	NAME
	PASSWORD
	RADIO
	RESET
	SIZE
	SRC
	SUBMIT
	TEXT
	TYPE
	VALUE
`<SELECT>`	MULTIPLE
	NAME
	SIZE
`<OPTION>`	SELECTED
	VALUE
`<TEXTAREA>`	COLS
	NAME
	ROWS

List   Elements
<DIR>   COMPACT
<DL>   COMPACT
<DD>
<DT>
<LH>
<MENU>   COMPACT
<OL>   COMPACT
                TYPE
                START
<UL>   COMPACT
                TYPE
<LI>   TYPE
                VALUE

Table   Elements
<TABLE>   ALIGN
                BORDER
                CELLSPACING
                CELLPADDING
                WIDTH
<CAPTION>   ALIGN
<TR>   cell.HALIGN
                cell.VALIGN
<TD>   COLSPAN
                ROWSPAN
                NOWRAP
                cell.HALIGN
                cell.VALIGN
<TH>   COLSPAN
                ROWSPAN
                NOWRAP
                cell.HALIGN
                cell.VALIGN

Client-Side Image Map   Elements
<MAP>   NAME
<AREA>   ALT
                COORDS
                HREF

NOHREF
SHAPE

Frame   Elements
<FRAMES>
    MARGINHEIGHT
    MARGINWIDTH
    NAME
    NORESIZE
    SCROLLING
    SRC

<FRAMESET>
    COLS
    ROWS

<NOFRAMES>

Special Symbols

Ampersand sign (&)	&#38;
Copyright sign (c)	&#169;
Greater than sign (>)	&#62;
Less than sign (<)	&#60;
Non-breaking space	
Double quote (")	&#34;
Registered sign (R)	&#174

Appendix B: Sample Web Site

(Please note: This is a fictional web site.)

First Page
```
<HTML>
<HEAD>
<TITLE>Hattori Properties</TITLE>
</HEAD>
<BODY>
<IMG SRC = "logo.gif" ALT="[www.hattori.com logo]">
<BR>
<BR>
<P>233 Alexander Avenue<BR>
Tall Tree, CA 94301</P>
<P>(415) 555-1212 phone<BR>
(415) 555-1211 fax</P>
<P>
Or via e-mail at <A HREF="mailto:hattori@rhattori.com">hattori@rhattori.com</A><BR><BR>
<HR>
```

<P>
Hattori Properties is a full service property management and real estate brokerage firm serving the San Francisco Bay area. Located in downtown Tall Tree, Hattori Properties is geared to serve the owner of smaller commercial and residential properties and has a staff of knowledgeable professionals, who work closely together. The small size of our company enables us to be flexible and to respond to the needs of both our owners and tenants on a <EM>personal</EM> basis.
<p>
We have grown steadily for the last five years with a balanced portfolio of office, retail, industrial, multi-family and single family properties from San Francisco to San Jose. <EM>Ninety percent</EM> of our business comes from client referrals.
<H2>Hattori Properties News</H2>
<UL>
<LI>
Helped the City of Tall Tree's Economic and Resources and Planning Dept. with its report <EM>Retail Trends in Downtown Tall Tree, 199x</EM>. The city won an award in a national competition for this report.
<LI>
Completed a consulting assignment for the Tall Tree City Manager's office on the <EM>Planned Community Zoning Process in Tall Tree</EM>.
<LI>
Represented buyer and seller of an apartment complex at Powell and Bush Streets in San Francisco in Oct. 199x. Hattori Properties will manage the property.
<LI>
Leased and now is managing a 33,000 square foot office building on Welch Road, Tall Tree.

```
</UL>
<H2><A HREF = "services.html">Services</A></H2>
</BODY>
</HTML>
```

Second Page

```
<HTML>
<HEAD>
<TITLE>Hattori Properties: Services</TITLE>
</HEAD>
<BODY>
<IMG SRC="logo.gif" ALT="[www.hattori.com
logo]" HEIGHT="150" WIDTH="150">
<BR>
<BR>
<P>233 Alexander Avenue<BR>
Tall Tree, CA 94301</P>
<P>(415) 555-1212 phone<BR>
(415) 555-1211 fax</P>
</B></UL>
Or via e-mail at <A
HREF="mailto:hattori@rhattori.com">hattori@rhat
tori.com</A><BR><BR>
<H1>Services </H1>
<P>
Hattori Properties is a full-service property
management and real estate brokerage firm
serving the San Francisco Bay area. Owned and
operated by the Hattori family for over ten
years, Hattori properties is well known for
its expertise as well as its personal service.
<H3>Tight Financial Controls</H3>
Tight financial controls are the key to a
profitable real estate operation in today's
market. Using state-of-the-art computer
software produce for property managers, Hattori
Properties can plan, analyze, control, and
```

evaluate the operating costs and income of your properties. We also send timely and accurate financial reports to all of our owners.
<H3>Enhancing Your Property Values</H3>
Our goal is to preserve and enhance the long-term value of your properties. We accomplish this by:
<UL>
<LI>Working with property owners in suggesting ways to increase cash flow
<LI>Monitoring capital expenditures
<LI>Supervising preventive maintenance with frequent site inspections
<LI>Analyzing and commenting on monthly and yearly financial statements
<LI>Preparing and monitoring annual budgets
<LI>Effective marketing and lease negotiations for vacant space
<LI>Constant monitoring of the surrounding real estate market
<LI>Responding to tenant requests in a timely manner
</UL>

<H2><A HREF = "hattori.html">Return to Hattori Properties Main Page
</A></H2>
</BODY>
</HTML>

Suggested Reading

Blanchard, K. and S. Johnson. *The One Minute Manager.* New York: William Morrow and Company. 1982.

Bolles, R. N. *What Color is Your Parachute?* Berkeley, CA: Ten Speed Press, 1992.

Burek, D. editor. *Encyclopedia of Associations.* Detroit: Gale Research. 1990.

Ferguson, M. *The Aquarian Conspiracy.* Los Angeles: J.P. Tarcher. 1980.

Ford, Andrew. *Spinning the Web.* International Thomson Publishings. 1995.

Gerberg, R.J. *The Professional Job Changing System.* Parsippany, NJ: Performance Dynamics. 1980.

Granovetter, M.S. *Getting Jobs: A Study of Contacts and Careers.* Cambridge: Harvard University Press. 1974.

Kanter, R.M. *The Change Masters: Innovation and Entrepreneurship in the American Corporation.* New York: Simon and Schuster. 1983.

Naisbitt, John. *Megatrends.* New York: Warner Communications. 1982.

Potter, B. A. *The Way of the Ronin.* New York: Amacom. 1984.

Raye-Johnson, V. *Effective Networking.* Los Altos, CA: Crisp Publications. 1990.

Ries, A. and Trout, J. *Horse Sense: The Key to Success is Finding a Horse to Ride.* New

York: McGraw-Hill Inc., 1991.

Rust, H.L. *Job Search: The Complete Manual for Jobseekers.* New York: Amacom. 1979.

Scheele, A. M. *Skills for Success: A Guide to the Top for Men and Women.* New York: Ballantine Books. 1979.

Sher, B. and Gottlieb, A. *Teamworks!* New York: Warner Books, Inc., 1989.

Von Oech, R. *A Kick in the Seat of the Pants.* New York: Harper and Row. 1986.

Welch, M.S. *Networking.* New York: Harcourt Brace Jovanovich. 1980.

Index

accountants	66	college advisers	52
acquaintances, social	61	college alumni	52
advisers, college	52	competing	159
advisers, professional	66	conducting letter-writing	
altruism	21,	campaign	85
alumni	52	consulting	157
appearance	135	contact sheet	76
articles	158	*Conversationally Speaking*	75
Bardwick, Judith	3	cooperatives	50
Bentley, Helen	62	co-workers	54
Bernstein, Paula	63	Crossen, Cynthia	16
Be Your Own Headhunter		customers	58
Online	123	dentists	66
Blanchard, Kenneth	23	de Oliveira, Paulo	82
Bolles, Richard	x	directories	68
books	158	distribution lists	129
Boolean searches	141	Dixon, Pam	123
bosses	55	doctors	66
building the network	31, 37	Dworkin, Gary	4
business associates	54	educational associates	46
business cards	73	*Effective Networking*	155
cards, collecting	73	e-mail	121, 125
career counselors	51	emoticons	132
career placement centers	49	empowerment	21
career web sites	143	*Encyclopedia of*	
casual acquaintances vs. good		*Associations*	69
friends as contacts	35	ethnic ties	15, 62
Chandler, David M.	137	expanding your network	68
Change Masters, The	14	externships	50
churches	60	family	39
classmates	48	*Family Ties, Corporate*	
clubs	60	*Bonds*	63
Cohen, Steve	82	favors	22, 104
colleagues	54, 122	fax machines	161
collecting business cards	73	flexibility	14

follow-up
   on interviews 102,
   phone calls 84, 94, 102
friends 42
Garner, Alan 75
Getting Jobs: A Study of Contacts and Careers 35
Getting to the Right Job 82
Ginn, Bob 80
goal orientation 17
Granovetter, Mark 35, 39
gratitude 23
Harragan, Betty Lehan 3
Harvard Univ. 2, 35, 81, 121
home page 138
hosting the function trick 76
How To Work a Room 122
HTML (HyperText markup language) 122, 148, 167
   list tags and more 151
   hypertext link 152
identifying your existing network 33
improving self-image 155, 160
informational interviewing 79
   follow up 102
   giving 110
   potential problems 102
   questions 99
   staying organized 107
instructors 47
Internet
   defined 113
   domain name 121
   domain type 121
   history 120
   privacy 128
internships 50
interviewing industry expert 97

interviewing, informational 79
introducing yourself 74
job
   interviewing vs. informational interviewing 82
   fairs (internet) 144
   placement centers 49
   samples, preparing 91
Johnson, Spencer 23
joining organizations 69
Kanter, Rosabeth 14
Kick in the Seat of the Pants, A 39
lawyers 66
leading a volunteer organization 159
letter vs. phone call 89
letter-writing campaign 85
listservs 132
managers 3, 54, 55
maximizing networking efforts 155
Megatrends 23, 34, 79
Merton, Robert 164
Milgram, Stanley 22
Mother's Almanac, The 28
Naisbitt, John 23, 34, 79
National Speaker's Association 157
naysayers 163
neighbors 63
nepotism 41
network
   building 37
   defined 12
   expanding 33, 66
   identifying 33, 38
   principles 13

Index

Networking	71	small business sites	
One Minute Manager, The	23	(Internet)	145
openness	14	social acquaintances	60
organizations, joining	69	societies, professional	70
Pearson, Dr. Judith	162	Society for Technical	
persistence	26	Communications	70
personal contact	27	sports	60
phone call vs. letter	89	staying organized	107
plateauing trap	3	STC	70
Plateauing Trap, The	3	subordinates	58
preparing résumé and job		suppliers	58
samples	91	support staff	58
professional advisers	66	Tandem Computers	11
professional societies	70	teachers	47
professors	47	teaching	156
Psychology Today	22	telephone call vs. letter	89
public office	159	thank you notes	24
public speaking	157	thinking globally	34
publishing articles and		Toastmasters	
books	158	International	75, 157
questions at informational		tracking contacts	56, 73, 107
interview	98	*Training Magazine*	164
Raye-Johnson, Venda	155	Treybig, James G.	vii, 11
researching person and		URL (uniform resource	
company interviewed	96	locator)	139
résumé, preparing	91	usenet news	134
Roane, Susan	122	vendors	58
running for public office	159	volunteering	69, 159
Running a Perfect Web		Von Oech, Roger	39
Site	137	web page / web site	122, 137
Sandler, Len	163	creating	147
Scheele, Adele	6, 16, 23	Welch, Mary Scott	71
schools	46	*Whack on the Side of the*	
self-disclosure	19	*Head, A*	39
self-fulfilling prophecy	164	*What Color Is Your*	
self-image	160	*Parachute?*	x
search engine	140	World Wide Web (WWW)	137
Skills for Success	6	*Working Woman*	16
		writing	158

To order additional copies of

It's Who You Know

Book: $14.95   Shipping/Handling $3.50

Contact: ***BookPartners, Inc.***
P.O. Box 922, Wilsonville, OR 97070
Fax: 503-682-8684
Phone 503-682-9821
Phone: 1-800-895-7323